From Ash to Fire:
A Journey of God's
Great Reversals

Cycle B Sermons for Lent and Easter
Based on the Gospel Lessons

I0151023

Heather Sugden

CSS Publishing Company, Inc.
Lima, Ohio

FROM ASH TO FIRE: A JOURNEY OF GOD'S GREAT REVERSALS

FIRST EDITION
Copyright © 2023
by CSS Publishing Co., Inc.

Library of Congress Cataloging-in-Publication Data (Pending)

Names: Sugden, Heather, author.
Title: From ash to fire : a journey of God's great reversals : Cycle B
    sermons for Lent and Easter based on the Gospel Lessons / Heather
    Sugden.
Description: First edition. | Lima, Ohio : CSS Publishing Company, Inc.,
    [2023]
Identifiers: LCCN 2023028377 (print) | LCCN 2023028378 (ebook) | ISBN
    9780788030826 (paperback) | ISBN 9780788030833 (adobe pdf)
Subjects: LCSH: Catholic Church--Sermons. | Common lectionary (1992). Year
    B.
Classification: LCC BX1756.A2 S875 2023 (print) | LCC BX1756.A2 (ebook) |
    DDC 252 /.02--dc23 / eng / 20230927
LC record available at https: / /lccn.loc.gov /2023028377
LC ebook record available at https: / /lccn.loc.gov /2023028378

For more information about CSS Publishing Company resources, visit our website at www.csspub.com, email us at csr@csspub.com, or call (800) 241-4056.

e-book:
ISBN-13: 978-0-7880-3083-3
ISBN-10: 0-7880-3083-3

ISBN-13: 978-0-7880-3082-6
ISBN-10: 0-7880-3082-5

PRINTED IN USA

Contents

From Ash to Fire:
A Journey of God's Great Reversals

While the smell of smoke typically brings up warm memories of campfires for me, such sensory experiences pale next to the frightening images of wildfire that have threatened communities around the world. We are being challenged by new realities of our planet in crisis, alongside the devastating effects of disease and isolation of the past few years.

Sudden change is generally not something the church handles well — or, at least, the church as most of us have known it in our own generation. But the stories of our faith, from Ash Wednesday through Holy Week and Easter and into the festival of Pentecost, represent both death and rebirth. We are called to remember the ancient story of Passover, recall the words of Jesus at the Last Supper and from the cross, find elation in an empty tomb, and ponder how the Holy Spirit still blows in our world.

Indeed, God is not done with us, and God is still moving in the church, just as this journey of holy time reminds us. But the nature of God's action, and the timing of God's action, defy all of our expectations, so that ash begins a journey rather than ending it, and fire spreads not destruction, but the building up and great expansion of the kingdom of God that transcends all barriers of language and division.

We are invited on this journey with Jesus. Some of the steps seem counterintuitive, and some of the paths seem to be dead ends, but it is on this road from ash to fire that true life is found.

Ash Wednesday
Matthew 6:1-6, 16-21

People of Ash

Have you ever seen ash fall from the sky? Have you scraped it off your windshield? Brushed it off of your doorstep? Smelled it in your own nostrils?

I had heard friends in the western United States describe what it was like to live through "fire season." I had been shocked by the devastating pictures of fire's destruction in other parts of the world. But I had never known that particular fear until a drought and fire came close to my own home one summer.

We know we cannot control the weather, but there is a particular helplessness that comes with drought. It is as if all imagination has been sucked out of creation. The grass looked like August in June. The trees dropped their leaves to survive a parched July rather than wait for the cooler nights of October. By the time the heat of August rolled around, it felt like never-ending déjà vu rather than the last days of the summer season.

In this extreme summer, animals seemed just as confused as we humans. I saw deer casually eating grass right at the roadside while cars whizzed by, and birds desperately searching for pools of water on which to land and seek relief. All of creation seemed dried out and drained of color.

Drought has a way of drying up our imagination, too. I remember wondering if rain would ever come, if heat would ever leave, and if the green land I remembered was just a fantasy, or if it could be coaxed back to life with the return of water-heavy clouds. It seemed that every day's forecast was already written months in advance, and nothing else was possible except oppressive heat.

The summer was brutal, but even the stark extremes of drought could not prepare me for the devastation of wildfire.

We all knew it was possible. We had heard talking heads on television warn of the risks of campfires and lightning. But from what we had experienced in the past, trees were known as shade providers and connected to deep wells of life, not fuel for a fire's unsatiable appetite.

One day, as these stories tend to always go, all of our perceptions of what should and could be changed. A wildfire started in a state forest and quickly spread throughout the night. Hardworking firefighters jumped into service, and the public, who had never paid much attention to such news, were now glued to updates on how contained this fire was from hour to hour.

"What did ten percent contained look like?" I wondered. What did it take to get to twenty and a slow jump to twenty-five percent? Why was it taking so long to see those numbers grow? And why did I feel confident when the number finally rose above half, when that still meant a large portion that was out-of-control?

Even as my mind concentrated on the numbers related to the fire, my nose, however, was gathering information of a different story. An uncertain haziness in the sky soon became a very real smell of fire. The smell grew to include an irritation in my eyes, and a tickle in my throat — a small hint at what was only beginning.

Because as the wind picked up, it seemed that a jet stream directly from the fire in the forest miles away to our town had opened up. The haze was now a thick fog — a stew of smoke and ash that seemed unstoppable. The smoke snuck into every crevice; the ash was coating every surface on which it fell.

I remember the dueling fears I felt that morning: the fear driven by the news on my television and phone, and the fear I experienced through my senses in the data they processed. One fear had a numerical value assigned to it, but the other was simply too real to rationalize in any fashion.

No, at some level, it did not matter what the official report said on the fire, because now I could smell it, taste it, see the ash dropping in front of me. Trees that had been living were now dust in my yard, on my car, covering my flowers. Ash can only come from death, and here it was — invading my everyday life.

I realize how lucky I am to have only smelled smoke and seen the ash of others' trees on my town. Unlike the many people who have lost homes, lives, whole towns to wildfire, I was only an observer of the ash that arrives en masse from a fire burning nearby. I knew enough, however, to be afraid. I knew enough to worry about when the ash would stop. I knew enough to know that I was not in charge, and that the smoke and ash would go wherever they pleased, while I was left to observe and learn.

Later that same day — the day the fire burned nearby — the day the smoke and ash arrived in my town — that very day, I drove a few towns over for work. And I remember driving through the thick cloud of smoke and ash until a different sort of horizon appeared. There was a sharp line front of me — where this ash-heavy cloud stopped, and blue sky remained.

How could such a clear line of separation exist? There was no smoke lingering over the homes of this town under blue sky. No irritated eyes or scratchy throats. No warnings to stay indoors. No ash on the sidewalk or covering the flowerbeds. No constant checking of television and phones for updates on what percentage of the fire was contained. No, this place seemed to know nothing of the fire destroying only miles away, and sending its smoke and ash blowing even more closely.

Even stranger than seeing this difference between smoke-filled areas and smokeless skies was the reaction of people when I asked them if the smoke bothered them. "What smoke?" they asked. Their minds were elsewhere; their worries on the familiar rather than the urgency of fire.

"How can this be?" I remember thinking. How can people living so near one another be affected so differently? How can the cares of one population occupy their entire minds, while their neighbors do not know that particular care at all?

Unfortunately there are few places in the world anymore that have not experienced the devastating effects of wildfire. We have all seen the stories, read the reports, prayed for the firefighters and the victims.

And yet headlines fade. The wind shifts. There are people and places that we so easily forget.

We know that life is full of up's and down's, and that no one can avoid pain in some form. And yet we also live in a world that always searches for clear skies, and hopes it can steer clear of every cloud. We know smoke goes somewhere, and we pray it does not come in our direction.

We cannot help but wonder: Why does fire strike in one place and not another? Why does ash fall on a particular town, house, family —

and seemingly miss the neighbor? Why does the wind blow in such a way that some folks cannot avoid smoke, while others cannot smell it at all?

But as today's liturgy makes it abundantly clear, we are people who know ash. We know what it looks like, feels like, how it smudges on our foreheads and drops down our faces. And today, ash marks us.

Our gospel today does not call for the imposition of ashes. In fact, in a certain way it seems to call for the opposite, as Jesus instructs us that when we fast, we should not "look dismal, like the hypocrites," but instead should keep up our regular appearances and go about our routines.

It becomes, then, rather odd to put ashes on our foreheads in such a way that the world cannot help but notice who is marked with a dusty cross today. Have we become the very hypocrites mentioned by Jesus, who promote their own piety over the deepening of their faith through spiritual practices such as prayer and fasting? Are we focused on appearing holier than others and standing out today? Or are we simply confessing a truth to the world that has claimed us, and which we cannot help but share?

It is possible to wear the ash of this day as a sign for the world to see our religious identity — a sort of public marker of devotion to tradition and practice. We might stand out as different in the world today, as we mix with other people — bearing a cross right there on our foreheads for everyone to see. But it is also very possible that by the very act of receiving this cross, we might now remember what all this ash is about.

Today, this ash marks us. The cross is not only the destination of Good Friday, but the smoky trail of this journey of Lent. We are choosing the difficult path directly into the reality of human suffering, acknowledging that ash is not only symbolic, but a natural part of creation.

We are people who do not only talk about the life, death and resurrection of Christ, but believe it in every fiber of our being. We hold that through baptism — through a cross marked on our foreheads, in water and today in ash — we have been joined to Christ's death and resurrection. We are people who have smelled the smoke, felt the soot on our fingers, cried at what has been lost — and somehow, someway, confess that there is still life to be found.

And that somehow this life found in ash is the most abundant life we have ever encountered. Marked with the cross of Christ, we are reborn. We are a community who confesses today that true life comes through this cross of ash we wear, and that the love of God is for all.

Our journey begins, and our journey continues, as we speak the truth of the ash, and this season of Lent which will lead us to life.

Wilderness for this Time

My grandmother worked as a secretary her entire life. She worked for Boeing during the war; she worked for a law firm and in a college business office; she even worked as a church secretary. She was good at her job: incredibly organized, a fast and accurate typist — back when we still used typewriters — and she had a memory like no one I have ever met, so that she could be told something once and recall it in precise detail years later.

These were all great skills that made her an excellent worker and always an integral part of any workforce. And these were all skills that spilled over into her personal life as well. She kept meticulous records of her vacations and had closets full of slide carousels marked with the date and destination of every trip. She was the official family genealogist, and made it a point to cut out every picture and article in the local newspaper that had your name or face on it. And she was known for her letters — always typed! — that she would send to friends and relatives far away and even close by in the same town.

After she retired from her career as a secretary, one of Grandma's favorite things to do was to have her grandchildren come over and talk with them in her living room. She would make a big point out of setting up an appointment with a specific time, and blocking off an entire morning or afternoon to spend time with us. It felt, once again, like Grandma was still running an office.

Looking back, I probably did not appreciate the time set aside to be with my grandmother as much as I should have. I know I failed to pay attention to her stories the way I should have paid attention. Instead of seeing the time together as a gift, I would often be wondering why my grandmother wanted to "book" so much time together in the first place.

But there are certain details of that time together with Grandma that I do remember. I remember the little side table next to her chair where she kept the mail, with her most recently received personal letters in their own little pile so that she could re-read them and share them with visitors. I remember how she would carefully turn on the lamp next to her chair before she began to read. And I remember vividly the one day when my grandmother happened to mention the book she kept, right there on the side table next to her mail.

The book was like a journal crossed with an address book, intended for someone's notes or lists. But in this book, my grandmother told me, she wrote down all the names of her friends and family who had passed away.

As she talked about the book, she looked through some of the pages, asking if I remembered Uncle Sig, or a cousin living in Norway I had never met. Some names were familiar, but many were not.

She continued with classmates from childhood, friends met during wartime, distant relatives that had no clear family tree connection to me. The distance of biology or time or even communication did not matter to my grandmother: once she learned of their passing, their names all went in her book.

"There were so many names!" I remembered thinking. I could not imagine how she could have ever known so many people, let alone have lost so many people.

Eventually she set down the book and looked off towards the window. "I'm the last one left," she said. "The last of the Mohicans!"

I do not remember what her face looked like as she told me about this book of names. I do not remember if she looked sad, or teared up. I do not remember if she even looked at me while speaking of this book, of if she wondered if I understood what she was saying.

What I do remember from that moment was thinking that I had seen a part of my grandmother's life that made me uncomfortable. "Were kids supposed to know this stuff?" I thought to myself. I kept quiet, shrunk down in my chair, and waited for my grandmother to move on to another topic of conversation. Whether she caught my reaction or not, eventually she did change the subject, and went on to talk about something less heavy than a book of lost loved ones.

Over the years, my grandmother brought up the book a few other times — never in detail — usually just to mention another friend or relative whose name had been entered. She never talked about the sea of sadness that book represented. She never showed me her tears, or asked me what I thought about either the book or the lives named inside of the book. We never discussed the grief that surrounded her.

I remember thinking that I should ask something, or say some words of comfort, but I did not know where to begin. And so silence was our exchange.

I have felt that same feeling as an adult, too: the sense of being so close to someone's pain, yet not knowing how to understand it, or how to help, or how to handle my own instinct to make the other person's pain go away.

Perhaps it seems as if I should have outgrown such a feeling of helplessness, or at least have a better way of responding when I encounter what is awkward and uncomfortable.

Many times we do not know how to react when we see the burden that another person carries, even if we are simply catching a glimpse. We do not know how deep the pain goes, or why it appeared at that moment, or what it will take to heal. We simply know that it hurts, as it reminds us of the burden we carry, too.

* * *

Our Lent begins with the story of Jesus in the wilderness: forty days when he is tempted by Satan. While other gospel writers like Matthew and Luke include details on what these temptations are and how Jesus responds, Mark simply tells us that it happens — and when it happens — just after Jesus' baptism by John, and before John's arrest. So that right between this high point of baptism, and this low point of John's arrest, come forty days of wilderness. A long stretch of time that Jesus spends with the wild beasts, and with angels who wait on him.

We are left to imagine exactly what this time in the wilderness looks like. While wilderness might sound to us like camping in the forest or hiking in the mountains, in the Bible it refers to a place outside of the safety of the world we know. The wilderness is a place of danger, of discomfort, of challenge.

We can assume the wilderness would test Jesus' survival skills. That he would have a lot of time without the comforts of home, family, and friends. That he would be left with his own thoughts, his doubts, his fears — and the challenge of figuring out exactly who he is and what he is called to do in his mission on Earth.

As much as we do not know about these forty days in the wilderness, we do know that this time in the wilderness is formative for Jesus. This time will somehow clarify Jesus' mission and purpose to himself so that when he emerges from this place and this moment, he will go to the Galilee and proclaim the good news of God. As Jesus declares, "The time is fulfilled, and the kingdom of God has come near; repent, and believe in the good news."

There is something about the challenges of the wilderness — about temptation — about the unknown itself — that give an urgency and purpose to Jesus' life and ministry. There is something about this time in the wilderness far away from the life he has lived on Earth up until this time that reminds Jesus who he is.

* * *

Wilderness can be chosen; wilderness can be found. Wilderness can also be a place we find ourselves without knowing how or why we got there, and a time in which we simply desire to get back to where we were before.

Like our gospel today, wilderness experiences can sometimes follow immediately upon an experience of certainty. In other words, just when we think everything is going great and our path is clear and certain, suddenly we are lost, struggling, confused.

For some, the wilderness is extreme loneliness. For others, it is economic uncertainty. Some have known sickness and pain, while others have anxiety they just cannot place, but still know that life is not how it used to be.

We all wonder how we got here, and what it all means — for ourselves, and for others. We catch glimpses of others' pain, and know that there are wildernesses all around.

We cannot fix or change the wilderness experience. We cannot shorten it for ourselves or others. But as people of faith, we can point to the model of wilderness experience in this gospel story we hear today.

As Jesus' own story shows us, life can follow this movement from assurance and certainty, to temptation in the wilderness. But the wilderness and the particular pain of temptation is not the end of the story. No, instead, Jesus' time in the wilderness seems to help clarify his mission and purpose.

When Jesus emerges from the wilderness, life is still not perfect. No, in fact, the story continues with news that John the Baptist has been arrested, a pivotal point in John's life that will lead to his own death for telling the truth.

Into this moment of wilderness for John and his followers, Jesus proclaims the good news of God. He announced that the kingdom of God has come near. He calls people to repent, and believe in the good news.

Where others must have felt certain defeat, where chaos and death's grip loom large, Jesus proclaims God's truth.

* * *

Wilderness in this time has taken on new meaning for our world. We who have lived through a pandemic could have never imagined before the year 2020. We who might look back and find it hard to believe it was true. We who even now question if we are safe, uncertain if the wilderness of sickness is behind us, or if we still have miles to go.

We are still living days outside of our comfort zones, with grief we could not have imagined. We have lost everything from our daily routines, to the lives of friends and family, to the gift of precious time with those we love.

What does it mean to proclaim the good news to the people of this time, this place, this world, this wilderness?

Rather than seek a new wilderness or see this gospel as a far-off dream, I wonder if Jesus might invite us to let go of our own need for certainty, and instead simply let him proclaim the hope of this moment. We can still repent. We still have time to turn to God. We are invited to see the kingdom of God — arrived in our own world — a Savior who does not shy away from brokenness, and always dares to proclaim truth.

Falling into Trust

Growing up in a small town, my church's youth group was a big part of my social life. The other youth were kids I had known since we were in pre-kindergarten Sunday School classes. My family knew their families; we went to public school together; I could even identify their parents' cars!

I liked my fellow youth group members, even if sometimes we probably got tired of seeing one another all of the time. If trust was an offshoot of familiarity, we had it covered.

Of course, trust is more complicated than simply spending time with people, even as time often grows trust. And trust — trust as related to faith — can be a difficult concept to define, let alone live up to.

A popular youth group activity when I was a teenager was the trust fall. The activity would begin with the adult leader talking about the need to trust God, and then segue into the physical activity of catching every youth group member as they fell backwards, thereby proving that we could trust one another and therefore trust God, even when we could not see where we were headed.

Sometimes the trust fall was relatively simple: the one designated person would cross their arms, close their eyes, and fall back into the arms of the other members of the group.

Sometimes the leader's confidence would bring us to falling back off of elevated positions like chairs or even a memorable time at camp falling off of a picnic table!

I guess it seemed like a good idea, merging a faith concept with physical activity and adding a splash of danger. But for me, it was terrifying. I was not a small teen, and all I could imagine was falling on top of every other member of the youth group, crushing them and landing flat on the ground.

Despite such a devastating fall never actually happening, I did have a very active imagination. I could picture the other youth snickering at me, rolling their eyes at having to catch me, even stepping away and refusing to participate with me as the one falling backwards into their arms. Even when the reality was that the rest of the group encouraged me and cheered me on and promised to catch me, I still found it hard to believe that this trust fall could happen for me like it did for the other youth. I was happy to catch others, but just did not want to go ahead with my own fall.

Finally, after lots of convincing, I did eventually agree to fall back — albeit with my own fears still in place. You see, I would always hedge my bets by bending my knees and trying to lower myself down as slowly as possible rather than just falling straight backwards without hesitation.

I wish I could tell you that no one ever got dropped in youth group. I wish I could tell you that my trust in people and in God was solidified through this faith exercise. I wish I could tell you I now have no trouble falling backwards from the highest heights! But I am human. Now, just like then, I would rather ease myself into trust rather than falling straight backwards.

The truth is that we are not so strong that we can catch everyone. The truth is that humans do fail. The truth is that we are not perfect, and that we make mistakes — even when we try to be perfect. The truth is that people get hurt in the ups and downs of life, no matter their perceived level of trust.

The truth is, we all have a hard time with trust — since our human experiences with trust cannot even come close to the trust of which God speaks.

We've skipped ahead a few chapters today to the 8th chapter in the gospel of Mark. And although eight chapters might not seem like many, by this point in Jesus' story, the disciples have already seen Jesus do amazing things. They have heard him preach and teach with authority — in a way that no one has ever spoken before.

The disciples have stood as witnesses to whom Jesus is, and they must be feeling good at this point in the gospel story: filled with awe at the leader they are following, filled with pride at being on the "Jesus team." Perhaps the disciples are even dreaming of the glory that they will achieve together.

Today's message from Jesus, therefore, must come as more than a bit of a shock. Jesus teaches them that the Son of Man must undergo great suffering and rejection, that he will be killed, and after three days rise again. Peter is so caught off guard, so bewildered, so opposed to what Jesus is saying that he actually takes Jesus aside to rebuke him. [Imagine rebuking Jesus!]

We do not have Peter's words of rebuke in our gospel text, so we do not know exactly what he said to Jesus. But we know that Jesus rebukes Peter right back, saying Peter is setting his mind on human things rather than on divine things.

We can imagine that Peter did not like Jesus' message that he was going to suffer and die. We can imagine that Peter thought he could correct Jesus and perhaps change his mind. We can imagine that Peter had a different vision for where this life of discipleship would go other than ending at a cross: the instrument of punishment, humiliation and death by the Roman Empire.

As Jesus turns to address the crowd with his disciples, he does not back down or retract or even soften his original message. Instead he broadens the message so that it is not just about him, but about the way of life he shows forth, and the fullness of life into which he calls all who follow him.

Jesus is adamant that the life of a disciple involves denying ourselves, taking up our crosses, and following Jesus. And that in order to save our lives, we must be willing to lose our life for Jesus' sake.

We have heard those words before. We know that this is the language of faith. We nod in recognition that as hard as Jesus' message sounds, it is familiar to us. We recite in acknowledgment that this is the way Jesus talks, and that, indeed, these words will come true with Jesus' own suffering, death and resurrection.

But even when we nod our heads — even when we repeat the words- we still find it hard to trust that this way of life that seems so counter to life as we know it IS TRUE life — that it is life meant for US.

To follow Jesus to the cross — to take up our own cross and follow him — is to enter into a way of life that we really cannot put into words. It is to give without expectation of reward, to serve even though we would rather rule, to go out to the margins rather than stay comfy at home, to love even when we know how much rejection hurts.

Words fail me when I consider what Jesus is asking of us. Words also fail me when I see people actually living the way Jesus asks us to live:

- People caring for their neighbors through gifts of food, clothing, and shelter. And the priceless gifts of time and a listening ear.

- People caring for neighbors they have never met — down the street, down in another state, across the world.

- People willing to carry a bit more of the burden of this life in order to ease someone else's burden — opening their eyes to how others are hurting, and asking what more can be done to help.

- People praying — knowing that the world is still spinning — still searching to be made into God's kingdom.

I have been blessed to meet many people in my life who have trusted in God so deeply that they are willing to take on a journey that sends them directly into the winds of opposition. Some are aware of the challenges they have chosen; some simply feel a calling to live a life of such complete trust they cannot really summarize what exactly it is all about.

Perhaps trust is about falling backwards and knowing that we will be caught. Perhaps trust is being honest about our fears and knowing when to ask for help from our community. Perhaps trust is leaning in to the stiff breeze that tries to blow us back, and somehow finding a way to keep going, often with the help of those around us.

I have been blessed to witness trust in action in many people I have encountered in my life. Some of them have been open about the role of faith in their actions. Others simply do what they feel called to do, without worrying about which categories of belief and hope they might fit into.

For me, this life of trust has often shown up in the shape of caregivers, particularly those caring for loved ones who are nearing the end of life. To keep safe someone who is afraid, to comfort someone feeling distress, to hold someone's hand and remind them you are there even when they cannot say your name out loud, to sit in holy silence with someone who is struggling to breathe — all of such a life of care is to agree to fall backwards into a great unknown.

Love shows up in those moments of caregiving — not only the love of devotion found in a committed relationship of marriage, family or deep friendship. No, the love of such care is trust itself — a kind of trust in the unknown that can only come from God.

Such trust learns — often through painful trial and error — that it cannot secure an answer to any question easily. And, in fact, trust in those moments cannot even feel its way through the questions that swirl around it. But trust gravitates towards love — shown through devotion, gentleness, and presence.

Perhaps the trust that accompanies faith is not so much being forced to fall backwards to prove its realness, but the community that stands together, arms linked, eyes watchful, ever ready to reach out and help whoever needs help. The folks who stood ready when I was an awkward teen, the folks who have caught me throughout life, the people I stand alongside now, and the Savior who calls us together — all of us in trust together.

We are each, and we are all, journeying to the cross — even if we still find it hard to trust. Even if we, like Peter, are quick to want to do it our own way. We go anyway — knowing that we cannot catch ourselves, but that God is waiting; God is walking with us; and God will gather many hands to catch us.

The Machinery of Faith

I often say that the best preparation for any pastor would be an apprenticeship in property management. No matter how large or small the church, no matter how many or few members willing to volunteer, no matter the stewardship program or financial resources of the congregation, it would still be useful for pastors to know how to maintain a building.

While many pastors cringe at the idea of leaky roofs or clogged pipes, it has never been the carpentry or plumbing problems that dismay me. No, for whatever reason, I seem to attract building problems of the heating and cooling variety.

It is always too hot and humid in the summer, and much too cold in the winter. When the air system does work, the people who are perpetually cold seem to sit right under the air conditioning vent, shivering with three sweaters on, with the perpetually hot under the blast of the heating system in the winter, sweating away.

I have experienced all sorts of friction related to the efforts of comfortable indoor temperatures. There have been fights over thermostats, locks put on thermostats, and time-frenzied stress and frustration at not being able to locate the key for the lock on the thermostat.

These issues, of course, all assume that the heating and cooling systems work, which itself can be the issue! No oil, no electricity, no coolant. Blocked ducts, wires chewed by critters, clogged drains, leaky tanks. Smells that are rancid, smells that are toxic, smells that simply do not smell "right." A boiler that decides to break down on Christmas Eve, and an air conditioner that only works Monday through Saturday and decides to malfunction every Sunday morning.

And while I have become accustomed to everything that can go wrong with a church's heating and cooling system, I am not skilled in the least at actually fixing these problems. Although I must say that my troubleshooting skills have improved considerably with much on-the-job training!

I have needed all of this training and then some in my recent dealings with an antiquated air conditioning system. "Cutting edge for its time" has become my equivalent of "designed to drive one as batty as possible."

Let me be clear: I realize I am very fortunate to have air conditioning at all in my church building. I also realize that there is nothing easy about cooling a church building that's large, with enormously high ceilings in the sanctuary. Our building also has some years in it, and was built in pieces over a long time span, with additions here and there and doors everywhere.

Considering all the obstacles involved in keeping such a massive air space cool, it is truly amazing the church has air conditioning at all! And all of these considerations have resulted in an air conditioning system that should have its own operating encyclopedia rather than just an operating manual.

To operate the system requires a key, which is hidden in a metal box. The key looks like a cross between a tuning fork and something a pirate would use to lock a treasure box. And this key is needed for the switch on a wall in the hall to turn the system on and off. Once the key is used to turn the system off, then another switch can be flipped to adjust the bellows and direct the air to the particular part of the church that most needs cooling. Only once the bellows are adjusted and re-positioned can you flip the original switch to turn everything back on again. Which is exactly the moment when you begin to fervently pray that all the steps worked in the right order and that cool air might actually begin to flow from the air vents.

As complicated as the air conditioning system sounds, it actually is not hard for other people to operate, once they learn how. And the system continues to work on hot and humid days, despite the many constraints placed upon it. But to someone who is not mechanically gifted — like myself — the whole process of simply turning the machinery on and off seems like I am joining a choreographed dance after skipping practice for a month. It is buttons and clicks, swooshes and rattles, vents and returns, cooling liquid and hot exhaust from a complex machine that I imagine looks, up close, like a magical contraption Leonardo da Vinci drew in his notebook four hundred years ago.

In other words, I do not really understand how our air conditioning works. But I do know it is important. I know that it can bring needed relief in our hot and humid summers. And I know it is frustrating when it does not work right — when it is too hot inside, or the cold air hits right where someone is sitting in the pew and sends them running for a sweater.

In case you couldn't tell, I find that way too much of my time and energy goes into making sure the church's air conditioning system works for a few hours on a handful of Sundays in any given year. And I am not even the one tasked with doing the actual maintenance and fixing of the machine! But I am one of the chief worriers, complaint hearers, and hand wringers.

I realize the air conditioner is just a machine to bring us comfort when in the sanctuary. And yet this overly complex and complicated system seems to symbolize more than just a simple machine.

No, like many things that operate in church spaces, its complexity seems to be inversely proportional to its necessity for worship, and yet directly proportional to its importance in the minds of church members. So much so, in fact, that often the first observation folks make on a Sunday morning in the summer is how well the air conditioning is working.

"Did you turn on the air conditioning?" will be asked upon entering.

"Is it working alright?" will be asked if the air seems a bit too humid or warm.

"Did you remember all the steps?" will be asked if my answer does not satisfy the first questions.

We tend to fixate on what we can grasp — even if we cannot fully understand it. And so the machinery of cooling hot and humid air takes on great importance. Even greater importance, it seems, than questions of how we are serving our neighbor, what discipleship looks like this day, why it seems like the church as an institution is dying, and what in the world we can or should do to keep the church going.

I know — I hear it, too. I can imagine that Jesus might have more than a few words to say to me about why I am so concerned about a building and its air cooling system. I can imagine that Jesus might have even more to say and show me in how to serve others rather than keeping myself comfortable.

Machines — like air conditioners, like boilers, like vans and buses, like lawnmowers and leaf blowers, like pipe organs and high-tech sound systems — all have a way of making us believe they can be mastered and therefore make us a better church. Also machines — like committee structures, rules and traditions, hierarchy and power systems, money and status — all have a way of making us believe they can be mastered and therefore make us a better church.

What would Jesus say if he entered our church today? Would he be comfortable with our machines? Or would he be apt to make a whip of cords, turn over our orderly tables, and drive about a change in our midst? Would we, at the very least, be awakened by the sound of Jesus' zealous arrival in our midst?

> *His disciples remembered that it was written, "Zeal for your house will consume me." —John 2:17*

Zeal is a word I associate with excitement, joy — happiness, even. But the zeal we hear about in our gospel today is one that sounds very different.

What is this zeal that consumes? That destroys? That has passion to such a degree that its burn cannot be stopped?

It is easy to point fingers at "other" people who believe in ideas with which we do not agree. We can call them brainwashed, irrational, or simply overly dedicated to a cause. But it is important to recognize ideas for which we are passionate, and issues which cause us great concern. It is a good thing to care, to dedicate ourselves to good causes, to want to work to make life better for all people.

But often the hot temperature of "zeal" seems out of place for church life, where we tend to emphasize self-control, order and even compliance.

When I hear of Jesus entering the temple today, consumed by zeal, it is natural to feel a bit uncomfortable at first. This image, this behavior, does not fit in with the image we have of a docile and gentle Jesus.

And yet we know Jesus is passionate about the truth. He will repeat over and over again to his disciples that they are to be servants. He will cross boundaries thought uncrossable to heal and forgive people of their sins. His love will be so all-reaching and so intense that he will die on a cross. His resurrection will destroy death forever.

Indeed, there is nothing lukewarm about anything Jesus does. So why do we insist on tempering Jesus' truth and making it more palatable? Why are we prone to the trap of focusing on the machinery of religion rather than the life, death and resurrection of Jesus Christ?

The church's experience with Covid restrictions can provide one window into our experience with the machinery of religion. In March of 2020, we went from regular Lenten worship that was marching orderly to Holy Week, to absolute unknowing. Facing a disease no one understood at the time, we shut down worship the way we "always" did worship. We scrambled to livestream, meet on computer screens, gather in parking lots, and greet one another from far distances so as to stay safe.

During Covid lockdowns, we also scrambled to connect through drive-by parades, cards and phone calls, and cheering on our first responders. We rushed to serve one another by donating food, furiously making cloth masks, and fervently praying for healing for names we knew and names we did not know.

Stripping away all of the "usual" aspects of church life was jolting and scary. It also showed that we did not have to do the "usual" stuff in order to worship. God was still present — even in and through ways we had never imagined God might be present before.

I do not want to equate Jesus' episode in the temple with the Covid pandemic. But I do recognize my own need to have tables turned, and to have Jesus wake me up to what worship is all about.

Surely God is present in ways and places I never imagined. And God continues to be present, as Jesus' life, death, and resurrection bring truth to us all. The buzzing of machinery might capture our attention, but it is Jesus' zeal that aims to capture our entire lives. May it be so.

Lent 4
John 3:14-21

A Cross that Bridges every Divide

I was sitting in a quiet room in my house, waiting for my cell phone to ring. I hoped it would stay quiet — that there would be no noisy distractions in the house for this important phone call — but also cherishing the quiet that came before the ring of the phone.

I knew the call would be a marker, dividing the time before it with all that would unfold following the call. I knew that the call was coming any second, and that there was no turning back now.

George's son had called me earlier that afternoon to explain that his father was not doing well. Things had been bad yesterday, too, but I still held out some hope for more time. Now there was just time to wait for the phone to ring, and bring its completion.

These were not the earliest days of the Covid-19 pandemic, but the holiday wave that happened in the first winter. There were still so many unknowns, so many "never befores," so many firsts we wished had never happened. Hospitals still had very strict visitation policies, and colored codes warned those of us on the outside of the hospital just how terrifying it was inside the hospital walls.

George had been in and out of the hospital and nursing home for several weeks due to long-term health problems. But now he was dying. His son called to update me on just how serious his condition was, and had arranged a phone call with me to offer a final prayer of comfort for patient and son.

A lifelong member of my congregation, George was one of those people you couldn't help but love when you met him. He was confident and opinionated; he was generous and would do anything for anyone who asked him to help.

He was also famously stubborn, refusing to leave his home and move into a long-term care facility; refusing to stay home when a virus raged through the community.

Now he was lying in a hospital bed, struggling to breathe, while a nurse held a monitor and camera in front of him so that he could see his son. His son told me that he would hold another phone up to the monitor on his side, so that his father could hear my voice praying, while at the same time his son could see his father to say goodbye.

What a strange world this was..... A man who loved to tell stories about chicken coops and unpaved streets now saying goodbye through a computer monitor.... George might have laughed at how very strange it was, or found the whole story impossible to believe if it had not happened to him.

When my cell phone rang, I jumped in my seat. I knew who was calling me, but I still acted surprised, my heart racing as I tried to calm myself down. With phone held to my ear, and phone held to computer, and computer lifted for patient, I read a scripture that I knew George loved. I prayed. I told him I would miss him. I recited to him, "Well done, good and faithful servant," and said, more to myself than him, "until we meet again."

There was silence. I decided to pray the Lord's prayer, which we three prayed together, each in our own way.

Maybe George looked up at the familiar prayer. Maybe his eyes stayed closed. His son did not tell me what exactly happened. But George took his final breath not long after our phone call ended.

I do not know if George's final vision on Earth was his son through the computer screen, or his nurse in the same room. He could have been looking at the monitors beeping in his room, or the fluorescent light above his bed. Perhaps George saw his wife or parents or son who preceded him in death. Maybe George saw a cross, or his childhood home, or maybe he saw the arms of his savior welcoming him home.

It still feels strange to me that there was separation between us when George died; that pastor could not retrace the baptismal cross on parishioner's forehead; that neither his son nor I could hold his hand to comfort him.

It has been a strange time of separation due to the pandemic. And yet the season of Lent reminds us that God erases every separation, and builds bridges over every chasm. Indeed, wherever there is separation, God finds a way to draw creation close.

* * *

This week's gospel includes the verse known as shorthand for the Christian message: John 3:16 — "For God so loved the world that he gave his only Son, so that everyone who believes in him may not perish but may have eternal life."

We know this verse because of its power and beauty: that Jesus is a gift of love from God to the world — the power of life over death.

But the verse is set within a larger story. In fact, it is part of a conversation between Jesus and Nicodemus. Remember Nicodemus? He is a leader in Judaism at the time of Jesus — a man who stands before others with authority and respect — a man who claims to have all the answers.

But it is Nicodemus who has come to Jesus under the cover of night because he has questions for Jesus. And he believes Jesus has the answers.

The gospel we hear today is part of their exchange. And that puts us at a little bit of a disadvantage because there is so much to unpack in just this short passage. But it is important to keep in mind that Jesus' words are in response to someone's questions — someone who is seeking truth — someone who is coming into belief.

Jesus even uses another biblical story to help Nicodemus, drawing on this image of Moses in the wilderness. This is a reference to Moses leading the Israelites to the Promised Land. When poisonous snakes bite the Israelites and they begin to die, God instructs Moses to make a serpent out of bronze and set it on a pole. Whoever is bitten by a snake must look at this bronze serpent and then they will live.

It seems like an odd reference for Jesus to make here to Nicodemus. It is an odd story of the Old Testament — especially if you are terrified of snakes. But it is also a powerful key to what Jesus is teaching Nicodemus about Jesus' own life, and death, and resurrection: "Just as Moses lifted up the serpent in the wilderness, so must the Son of Man be lifted up, that whoever believes in him may have eternal life."

Jesus will be lifted up on a cross — an instrument of his suffering and of his death. But the cross that kills him will not hold him. Neither will the anger of the crowd, or the fear of the religious authorities trying to protect the old ways. No, not even the most powerful empire in the world will accomplish their purpose by the execution of Jesus on a cross. Instead, the very instrument of his suffering and death will also lead to his triumph in the resurrection.

And so this cross that we carry out for worship each Sunday — this cross that we identify as emblematic of our faith — this cross that has become our shorthand for all that we believe — this cross carries with it both life and death — intersected and transformed in the person of Jesus Christ.

Look to the cross, and we will see humiliation and grief. Look to the cross, and we will see pain and suffering. Look to the cross, and we will see how empire and evil operate. Look to the cross, and we will see all the old ways dying in darkness, and light breaking through to a new way. Because the cross that kills is also the cross that grants true freedom. When we look to the cross, we will see God's love — so powerful that God gave his only Son so that we might all have life.

This cross is the bridge that moves death to life, and opens the world to the truth that God will not be stopped by anything — even by death.

So that when we fear the world is perishing, when we feel unloved and alone, when we are separated by sin and all the divisions of this world which dominate our daily stories — it is then we might look to the cross and see life.

I wonder where we might look today, and where the cross shows up in our own lives?

I know that during the pandemic time of isolation, the cross was very real to those who were alone in hospitals, and to their loved ones who felt helpless at home. The cross was found on the faces of overwhelmed doctors and nurses and hospital staff who were trying to keep people alive and give them both peace and hope. The cross was in the hands of all who were praying — despite feeling so helpless — praying because they felt helpless — praying knowing that God was present and listening, even when the words of prayer did not always come out right.

The cross is wherever we look, wherever we see, wherever we trust that God is at work bringing healing and wholeness and salvation to us all. Often times, the cross is in the very places we are hurting.

When we look to the cross, in our suffering and in our hope, we will see love — the great eternal love of God from which we can never be separated.

Lent 5
John 12:20-33

Seeds of Faith

Happy St. Patrick's Day! It might be the 5th Sunday in Lent, but it is also the day when the whole world can claim to be Irish. Get your corned beef and cabbage ready: it's time to celebrate!

St. Patrick dates all the way back to the 5th century, and so it is difficult to pinpoint the historical details of his life. But the stories of this early saint of the Christian church have been passed on for generations not just in Ireland, but around the world.

Patrick, so the tale goes, grew up in a Christian family in Britain. As a teenager, he was stolen by Irish raiders and sold into slavery in Ireland. Patrick was assigned to care for the animals, where he spent time thinking about the Christian faith he had been introduced to as a child.

Patrick prayed and committed his life to Christ. After six years in slavery in Ireland, he had a vision of a boat waiting for him. He escaped from his master, found the boat at the shore, and made it back to Britain.

Obviously, Patrick's escape from slavery and voyage back to Britain was not the end of his story. He studied Christianity while home in Britain, became a priest, and received another vision: this one telling him that he was to go back to Ireland as a Christian missionary.

And the rest, as they say, is history. Patrick taught the Irish people about the Holy Trinity by using the example of the shamrock. He brought people to Christ and taught them how to live a faithful life. And, of course, supposedly he chased all the snakes off the island, too.

We celebrate all of this on March 17th. We say we are all a little Irish because of a saint who was never Irish himself, and yet has come to embody all the strength and perseverance that we associate with the Irish people.

In the church, St. Patrick symbolizes a particular kind of faith that led him to face difficulties in life head on: not with bitterness or fear, but with an openness to God's word and vision and voice, and the courage to follow.

We know the story of St. Patrick; we celebrate the story of St. Patrick. We wear the green and look for the shamrocks and eat the festive food of the day. But as we consider Patrick's incredible story today, we also have to wonder why. Why in the world did his story turn out that way? Why would Patrick, after escaping slavery in Ireland, then go back to Ireland? Why would someone who follows a vision across the sea, then go back to the very spot he had just left? Why would he try to heal the people who had hurt him?

Why, indeed, was freedom for Patrick found not in a physical location, and not in breaking the bonds of his own captivity, but only freedom in service to Christ? What was it about the nature of this freedom he discovered in his faith that compelled him to free others?

Perhaps this all seems a bit too deep considering that parties have already started, rivers have been dyed green, and people are dressing up as leprechauns today. But the convictions of Patrick's life truly are to be admired today, and lifted up for us all.

How might we listen to God's voice today? What courage do we need in order to follow where God is sending us? And what is it about now — at this exact moment — that just like Patrick, our faith is calling us to something we could never imagine for ourselves?

"Very truly I tell you," Jesus says, "unless a grain of wheat falls into the earth and dies, it remains just a single grain; but if it dies, it bears much fruit."

Jesus says these words to a crowd gathered to hear him. This group includes his disciples and others who are in Jerusalem during this holy season and are curious to hear Jesus speak. We meet a group only identified as the Greeks, who express their wish to simply see Jesus in what will become his final week on earth.

Now what Jesus says in today's gospel makes sense in light of what we know will happen that week: Jesus will die, and out of his death will come true life. But as Jesus himself reveals in this passage, what is about to occur is fraught with tension. Jesus even tells us that now — in this moment — his soul is troubled. And yet he will not ask to be spared what is to come, but, as he says, "It is for this reason" that he has come to this very hour.

What is it about this time that makes Jesus so confident in what is about to happen to him? Certainly Jesus has a sense of purpose, which really is rooted in his sense of identity. Jesus knows he is God's Son. Jesus knows he is God's expression of love to the world. Jesus knows that he will draw all people to himself.

And yet — even with such certainty — there is this moment — so loaded with meaning and so fraught with tension — a time so heavy with God's presence and power — that the weight of it seems to all be on Jesus' shoulders.

Rather than run the other way, Jesus identifies this moment as the time to plant the seed of salvation — of death that will bring forth eternal life.

The fancy word is "kairos." *Kairos* is the Greek word used to describe time — not as simply the progression of hands on the clock, but time that is measured by the weight of the moment. *Kairos* is the right time, the critical time, the opportune time.

For whatever reason, God chose this moment described in our gospel today as the *kairos* for his own son to bring salvation to the world.

We have probably experienced our own moments in time that weigh heavier than others. Perhaps it was a moment where time seemed to stand still. Perhaps it is a moment that marked a distinct change in our lives, so that now we can mark our story's progression with "before" and "after" related to this particular moment.

Many times we might not realize the moment is deeply meaningful until after it has passed. But we all know what it means to wait; to ponder when; to be in a holding pattern or frozen in our "starter stance," anxious to begin.

To identify the right time is never easy. But we follow the example of our leader, who never tires in showing us the way.

* * *

I grew up on a farm in northern Minnesota. We grew small grains back then — mostly wheat and sunflowers when I was a kid. And I can still remember that spring was a worrisome time for farmers back then — and I'm sure it still is worrisome today.

It seems like it should be simple: spring comes, the weather warms, you put the seed in the wet ground, and then you sit back and watch it grow. But a seed actually can be pretty fussy. In order for a seed to sprout and grow, it needs to have the right temperature in the soil, and just the right amount of moisture. If it's too dry or too cold, the seed will never sprout. And if it's too wet, you can't get the tractor out in the field for one thing, but the seed can also rot in the wet ground.

Conditions have to be just right for the seed to swell and shed its outer shell, take root, and shoot up new life from the ground. And it takes an experienced farmer to know the right time to plant — to know how to be patient and to wait through a false spring. To wait for exactly the right conditions. And to know to work like crazy and get the crop into the ground in a hurry when the conditions are right.

Some farmers might tell you that's why they pray a lot. Some farmers might say that's why they worry a lot. All farmers will admit that even with all the advances in science and technology, it is still a miracle to watch a tiny seed grow into a mighty plant and produce seeds of its own in great abundance.

When Jesus speaks of a grain of wheat dying in the earth, it sounds like a pretty harsh way of describing the planting season! But the example holds true. There is risk in planting a seed, and yet not planting the seed produces no result.

It is only in going ahead with the planting — putting the seed into the earth — watching and waiting for the sprout to emerge from the ground — that the seed might grow and produce its fruit.

Although Jesus is troubled by what he is to face as he nears the cross, he also seems to sense that this is the time. And while his death is gruesome and his suffering undeserved, the life that emerges from the tomb is love beyond anyone's understanding.

As we near the end of our Lenten journey this year, as we approach the foot of the cross and rest in its awful shadow, as we are reminded of St. Patrick's great courage and service, as we consider the seeds we might be preparing to plant, the enormity of this time can seem quite overwhelming. But it is God who leads us; indeed, our call to service begins again right now through the example of our Lord and Savior Jesus Christ.

The Not-So-Easy Discipleship Trail

Palm Sunday for me is the beginning of a journey. There's a physical journey, as Jesus enters Jerusalem on a donkey with his disciples, and we can join in with our own hosannas. There is also a spiritual journey, as we enter into the events of Holy Week and Jesus fulfills his purpose on earth.

There's something really exciting about a journey. Call it a trip, a trek, a hike, a parade, a quest — a journey is a movement from one place to another. And a journey is something for which we need to prepare before we begin.

So today, as we are asked to join the procession into Jerusalem — as we are asked to join Jesus ' journey — we will discover that this turns out to not just be a journey of physical distance, but a journey that reveals who Jesus really is. And joining this journey — following Jesus — also will reveal who we really are.

A few years ago we took a family trip to Utah, and went to Arches National Park, which is renowned for those beautiful stone arches that are shown on the Utah license plates. The visual landscape is surreal — stunningly beautiful.

One of the fun things you can do there is go on a hike through that amazing terrain. There are several hiking trails throughout the park, ranked easy, moderate, or difficult. So when we were out there, I thought it would be fun to take a hike as a family. And so we got a map of the park with the hiking trails marked, and spoke to someone at our hotel about what would be a good hike to take.

Now I wasn't completely foolish — I knew that with young children, I better pick an easy hiking path. But in my mind, easy meant just that — easy. We should be able to wander out of the car, see something nice, and then go back to the car without breaking a sweat.

Seemed reasonable. Except it is desert out there in southern Utah. It is hot out there. And people who hike know what it takes to be prepared for a hike: taking plenty of water, and sunglasses, and sunscreen and a big ol' wide-brimmed hat.

That's what experienced hikers know. But that's not what weekend hikers — or tourists from New Jersey — necessarily know.

And so the "easy" hike that I picked out with the person at the hotel was not quite the "easy" hike I had in mind. I did bring water — one bottle I found in the car — for the four of us. And I think we had sunglasses, even if some of us left them in the car. To my credit, it was cloudy when we got out of the car.

No surprise here: the "easy" hike turned out to be not so easy. It was really hot, and really sandy, and steep and rocky and not a short distance at all. And I still don't understand: since when does an "easy" hiking trail go over boulders and down into deep dry riverbeds?!

I'm just glad we didn't try the difficult stuff — or even the intermediate hike, for that matter.

I learned that you have to be careful when you set out on a journey. Of course, you need to be prepared. But you also need to listen to what people are telling you. And you need to consider the source, as what is "easy" to some might not seem so easy once you get down the path.

This year's entrance into Holy Week begins with our worship today. Palm Sunday is usually a joyous Sunday. Even if we read the Passion narrative, which tells us what is about to happen to Jesus, we still get caught up in the palms, and the egg hunts, and the preparations for Easter.

We love the joy of the hosannas so much that we might forget those words of joy are actually words that plead for God to deliver us. We might overlook that our king rides on a humble colt, and forget that the crowds who welcome him will soon shout for his crucifixion.

In fact, it turns out that there is nothing easy about this journey Jesus invites us to join.

We know that the journey of discipleship is not easy. And yet we had hoped it would be. We had all hoped that the biggest obstacle we would face as church was paying off the mortgage, or getting our rambunctious kids to sit still. We had hoped that the biggest challenge we might face would be over contemporary music, or the best way to distribute communion.

We had hoped that we could keep sickness and death far away, and that faith would not demand too much from us.

We all sort of hope we signed up for the easy discipleship trail.

Suddenly, without warning, this journey with Jesus has become very real.

Which Jesus has been telling us all along. He did not promise it would be easy. In fact, as this week will show us, he rides into Jerusalem to end up betrayed by his friends, humiliated by crowds who once cheered him, and executed between criminals on a cross.

We do not observe our gospel today as a silent audience. No, this story is too important, too life-changing, too terrible, and too beautiful for us to simply sit back and watch.

Today's gospel demands that we pay attention. It draws us in as we are invited to Passover celebrations. We can smell the powerful aroma of nard, as the alabaster jar is broken and expensive perfume poured out upon Jesus. We hear the silver coins jingling in the purse Judas carries. We sit at the table with Jesus and the disciples and recall our own communion with him.

We hear Jesus praying in such a powerful way that we wonder how he went through with obedience to his Father's will.

We might also feel frustration at the disciples who fall asleep, and shock at Judas' betrayal. The violence of the soldiers who arrest Jesus, the disciples urge to respond with violence, seem all-too-familiar in our world. Our hearts drop as the disciples desert Jesus and flee, and Peter's actions might have us recoiling in shame.

When the crowd shouts, "Crucify him!" to Pilate, we cannot believe how people who welcomed Jesus with palm branches could have shifted their allegiances so quickly. We turn away at the flogging of Jesus, and we weep at his innocence put on trial. We know that fear is now in control, but we had hoped that this time could have been different.

It is mocking and spit that meet our king rather than honor and praise. The purple cloth and crown of thorns are for pain and insult, not the glory he deserves. But despite the hatred all around him, Jesus will turn these symbols into signs of service in his kingdom.

In his final earthly journey, Jesus will carry his own cross, with the help of a passer-by named Simon. While the physical journey would be excruciating for anyone who had been tortured like Jesus, the words of violence all around him must have hurt even more.

Truly this journey to the Golgotha is not measured by steps, but by the betrayal and desertion of all who followed him. Cheers of hosanna have turned to jeers of death; people who promised to follow him anywhere are now nowhere to be found. Even the criminals killed alongside Jesus taunt him in his agony.

Of course, we cannot help but wonder what we would have done under such circumstances. Would we have risked our own safety to be near Jesus? Would we have followed at a safe distance? Would we have stood nearby to watch and listen?

Could we have joined in on Jesus' journey? Or is this a day when we simply stand in awe of how great our Savior's love is for us?

I find that words are hard to come by when I attempt to explain what this week means to our faith. I struggle to comprehend what it means to my personal faith. But I know that only Jesus could walk this journey — not only to the cross, but to bridge the chasm of sin that engulfs us and keeps us from being close to God.

Jesus' journey will mean more to some of us this year than ever before, because of what we have seen and experienced in our own lives. We do not have to understand all the emotions we feel. But we are asked to follow along, and to not shy away from seeing and smelling, listening and experiencing all that Jesus' journey will bring.

No, it is not the easy path. But we also know that this is the path that will give life meaning. This week, through holy story, through singing and silence, through our presence alone and together, through prayer and through service, we will realize how much we need one another, how much we need faith, and how much we need a Savior.

So let us go now to Jerusalem and join the holy story that is our story, too.

Maundy Thursday
John 13:1-17, 31b-35

People Who Remember

Some years ago, I got to visiting a man in my community "who could use a visit," as I was told. His wife has had dementia for many years, and because of his caregiving responsibilities, the man is pretty isolated. He cannot leave the home out of fear for his wife's safety — that she might wander off, or fall, or simply forget where she is.

I like visiting this man. He lights up when he tells me all of his wild and crazy stories from his younger days when he lived in a wild and crazy place. He also lights up simply because he doesn't get too much company these days, and he delights in having anyone stop by to offer him company.

His wife's dementia has progressed so far that she cannot speak any more. Most of the time, she just sleeps, and doesn't even open her eyes when someone walks in the room and tries to talk to her.

The irony is that she used to be an incredibly active woman: not only raising her children and running the household, but also being an incredible cook, even doing some catering on the side. I have heard other people tell stories of her food: how she thought nothing of cooking for hundreds of people, how everything was always homemade, how she put love and care and pride into everything she made and served to people.

When I talk to her husband, he likes to remember those days when the house was always jumping with children and work and activities, with holidays and company and big special meals. I asked him once what he missed most from the days when his wife cooked: was there a particular dish, a particular meal, a special dessert that she used to make and that he now really misses?

He thought about the question for a little while, and then answered, "No. I don't miss any dish she used to make."

"Really?" I asked. "Isn't it hard to cook for yourself? You must miss all that good home cooking!"

And again he said, "No. I don't miss the food. I miss the conversation. I miss sitting at a full table. I miss hearing her yell at me that dinner was ready. I miss the fights we used to have. I miss hearing her worry about what the children were up to at school. I miss her asking me for money."

"No, I don't miss the food," he continued. "I miss the words. I miss her… even though she's sitting right next to me."

"How is it," he asked, "that someone can be right here, and yet far away at the same time?"

I did not have an easy answer for him. But I tried to listen. I tried to let him paint a picture of the person his wife was — her activities and interests — even as she could not find words to speak for herself. I tried to create a space where he could speak of his love for her — not just in the days gone by, but in the days in which he now cared for her.

We know that no one can escape the march of time. Some of us are blessed with good health and sharp minds for many years. Some of us know illness and suffering sooner than others.

We remember what was. And rather than let memory slip into nostalgic longing for the past, we have the opportunity to remember the past in powerful ways so that it might shape our present reality.

We are, after all, people who remember. A reality and a ritual that make this evening particularly powerful for our community.

This evening's service marks the beginning of the three holy days leading up to Easter. And the special holiness of these days is marked by tradition within each of our congregations: worshipping together; sharing the sacrament of communion at the Lord's Table; hearing the story of Jesus' betrayal, trial, and death; stripping the altar and sanctuary of all its adornments; singing songs of faith; and sitting in silence as we recall the ancient memory of faith.

Tonight we remember and celebrate the Last Supper. We will hear of the first Passover as the slaves of Pharoah will leave Egypt and become the Israelites of the Promised Land. We will hear of them eating together before quickly escaping to the wilderness, and how years later, Jesus and his disciples will go to Jerusalem to remember and celebrate the Jewish festival of the Passover.

As faithful Jews, they will gather around a table, with bread and wine and food, and with their prayers of tradition, they will not only remember the story of the Passover, but will begin a new story. There will be talk of betrayal as well as the demonstration of love through service, as Jesus washes his disciples' feet.

As Paul tells us later in 1 Corinthians, at this very same meal, Jesus will take a loaf of bread, give thanks, break it and say, "This is my body that is for you. Do this in remembrance of me." And then in the same way the cup of wine as his blood, in remembrance of him also.

There are layers of remembrance going on this evening: layers of history as we remember what Jesus also remembered, layers of history as we remember what Jesus' earliest followers remembered in breaking the bread and sharing the cup.

Meals are important to every culture, every faith, every family and tradition. And so tonight, as we enter into these holy days, we also begin with a meal.

And we will hear the same words Jesus passed on to his disciples, carried through all the generations of the faithful to us who now gather in this place tonight. "This is my body," we will hear as we see the bread. "This is my blood," as the cup is lifted up.

The food and drink are important, but the person whose presence they carry is even more important. Jesus himself will join us at the table this evening. Jesus himself is present at this gathering. Jesus himself will enter into our lives with his love and grace and blessing.

We know that. We confess that. We believe in Jesus' presence. And yet sometimes we need to be reminded of the holy presence that is amongst us here and now. We need to retell the holy story, and remember our own holy story. It is also our time to be honest about the hungers we still carry that we bring with us tonight.

One of the hungers I often hear is something like hope pointed backwards. Not quite nostalgia, not quite time machine, not quite regret, it is more like a generalized grief over the past. Sometimes in church life, I fear we have perfected this sensation, wishing for the time when we remember church and society as very different from what it is now.

Perhaps we even recall stories of packed church buildings, pews of bouncing babies, manners and respect in abundance, and kindness as social currency. We are keen to tell these stories of our glorious past, with a twinkle in our eye for the good old days.

I like those old stories, too. And I tell plenty of them.

But I am drawn this evening to Jesus' ability to take a story from the past — in this case, the story of Passover — and give it new life without taking away from the glories of its retelling. I wonder if we could learn from such an example. I wonder if we can be so passionate about being people who remember — remember this holy night — that we not only recreate it, but that we allow this night's particular passion to inspire our own faith.

Because at its heart, this particular Holy Thursday is one of such powerful memory that when we tell the story of Jesus, we cannot help but know he is present — right here, right now, right here amongst us. When we eat this bread, when we drink this cup, when we continue to find ways to love one another, Jesus is truly present with us, and we are his disciples.

So enter into the fullness of our service this evening. This evening's Holy Thursday worship is a chance to remember and reflect, to hear and appreciate the layers of history, to eat and drink and be filled as we move forward into these holiest of days. It is our time to be fed once again.

Destroying Every Separation

Today's gospel has an abrupt ending to the story of Jesus we have heard so far. Even though I've heard the story many times before, I am still always shocked by the ending. How could it end this way? How could someone so full of life have his life so quickly ended? How could a person who was so popular that he couldn't get away from mobs of followers now be hanging on a cross alone?

The throngs that he fed, the crowds that listened to him teach, the many he healed and who witnessed his miracles, and even the twelve disciples who were his closest confidantes have denied, abandoned, and even betrayed him.

Indeed, the familiar characters of most of our gospel stories have been replaced in the end by peripheral characters like Simon of Cyrene and Joseph of Arimathea.

So who is left to follow Jesus to the bitter end and stay by his side even during his awful death? Different gospel writers list slightly different groups of people, but they all attest that there is a group of women who stand by Jesus to the end, and the gospel of John tells us that one of these women was Jesus' own mother, so that the one who brought him into this world sees him leave it as well.

While there is lots of speculation, not much is really known about Mary, the mother of Jesus by the way of hard facts. We hear in the Bible that she is young and engaged to a man named Joseph when she is visited by an angel and told she will carry the son of God. That's the story we're familiar with, and we're happy to give her a central role at Christmas time, and a central place in our nativity scenes where she can be honored and celebrated.

The gospel writer Luke at least gives Mary a song of praise when she finds out she is pregnant, but often she is in the background of stories, watching and waiting, and simply named for her role as mother.

With just a little imagination, we can fill in the blanks of some favorite Bible stories that she appears in with small parts. There are the typical mother stories, like when she gets upset that Jesus runs off to the temple as a young boy without telling his parents where he is going, and the time she nags her son at the wedding at Cana to help out the newly married couple when the wine runs dry. These episodes paint her as a very typical mother — one that we can relate to either from our own experience of being a mother, or certainly of having a mother.

We know that she is strong — not just from what we are told in the Bible, such as her dedication to follow her son everywhere, even to his death, but also from what is not said. To our knowledge, she does not publicly protest what she knows Jesus must do in traveling to Jerusalem and death on a cross.

In our gospel, Mary is silent in her anguish of losing a son, and in the particularly devastating anguish of losing her son in such a violent and public way. Mary sees people hate her son — turning against him, spitting on him and humiliating him. None of us can imagine such pain.

Because of what is not said about Mary in the Bible, there are many legends surrounding her that have sprung up in the church. Christian legends are stories not recorded in the Bible, but they are still ancient and have been passed on from the early days of the church. No matter what you choose to make of them, at the very least, they are helpful in hearing what early Christians said and thought about Mary.

There is a certain legend about Mary, the mother of Jesus, that I think is especially helpful today, as we witness this devoted mother who stands in silence and watches her own son be crucified.

The story goes that in Mary's early days — before she was a mother, before she was engaged to Joseph, while the world did not yet speak her name and she was just a young Jewish girl whose parents were trying to figure out her future, Mary was an apprentice of sorts, who worked as a weaver in the precincts of the Temple in Jerusalem.

As we know from Jesus' own criticism years later, the temple was not only a holy place of priests and prayer and devotion, but it was also a busy place, and even a business place, where the business of changing money and the buying and selling of animals for sacrifice took place.

Mary was just one of many weavers in a sort of boarding school at the temple, where they worked to accomplish all the weaving that temple life required. There was weaving to be done in making the priest's special garments, and probably more everyday weaving for regular temple needs. But there was one very special weaving task that had to be accomplished at the temple: the weaving of the curtain that surrounded the holy of holies — the long purple and scarlet veil that separated the holiest place in the temple from the rest of the people of God and their activities in the temple.

The holy of holies is another great religious mystery, because the only person who really knew about it was the high priest. He was the only person who was ever allowed to go inside, and that was only once a year, on the day of atonement, when after much religious ritual and fasting and prayer, he could go into this place that housed the ark of the covenant. Once inside the holy of holies, the priest would call upon the name of God, and thereby ask God to forgive the sins of the people of Israel.

This place of holiness was believed to be where God himself resided — a God so magnificent and terrifying that no ordinary human being could call upon him or encounter him in that spot. Only the high priest could meet God on behalf of the people — and only on that one day. At any other time, the curtain was there to keep God separate — to divide God from the people — to keep sin and all the wordly business that we carry from interacting and possibly upsetting God.

Imagine, then, the weight of the task the young girl Mary has been assigned. It is she who will weave this veil. With the finest threads, she will create a cloth worthy of marking the line between God and humanity.

But something happens to Mary — her life is interrupted, which, as we know, will continue to happen throughout her life. An angel of God appears to Mary, and tells her that this is not her fate — she is not meant to weave this curtain. God has other things in store for her. She has an even more important task that God will reveal to her at a later time.

Mary leaves the big city, she leaves her calling at the temple, and she goes back to her simple country life in the backwater town of Nazareth. And indeed, she soon finds out that God has something very important in mind for her.

Today, as Jesus breathes his last, as the sky is darkened and the clock strikes 3:00, the curtain of the temple is torn in half, from the top all the way to the bottom. The work of the weaver is destroyed just like that, and the holy of holies is exposed as the curtain that divided it from the people comes undone.

Jesus's death does indeed not only tear in half the curtain separating the holy of holies: by defeating death itself, Jesus will destroy every separation between God and creation.

Mary stands as witness today at the foot of the cross. While the truth of resurrection's triumph is not yet fully revealed, today she stands grieving her son. No, she does not stand alone. The gospel in John tells us that other women, including her sister, stand with her. Noticing the disciple whom he loves also in the crowd, Jesus calls his mother to love him as a son, and Mary as the mother of the disciple. It is a touching human moment, of not wanting his mother to be alone.

Yet no matter who stands with Mary, there is deep grief and anguish on this day of Jesus's death. There is a loneliness — a separation, even — that comes through suffering and witnessing suffering.

Except Jesus will not allow the separation to be the final word. Even as death takes hold of his physical body, he refuses to let his spirit be weighed done by physical pain, mental fear, or emotional anguish. Instead, he turns over his spirit to God.

I have tried to wrestle with what this means; how we should understand Jesus' words; what lesson there is to gain. But the more I ponder what happens on Good Friday, the less I think I understand.

And I think that is probably the point. As human beings with rational minds and the full weapons of reason and science at our disposal, we can sometimes fool ourselves into believing that we are at war with death — indeed, that we can triumph over it all by ourselves.

Good Friday shows us that even Christ died. And as we sit here at the foot of the cross, we are tempted to run away — or at least to try and not think too much of exactly what Christ is going through. To think of his death — to think of death in general — is painful. We can't fix this problem. We can't prevent or outrun it. We can't even explain it. We can only weep at the suffering Jesus endures, and the senseless loss of an innocent life.

We know that when we leave here today, much of the world will seem oblivious to what has happened on the cross. The world goes on — working, shopping, laughing. The world also goes on with pain that many feel they must hide. The world goes on, pretending death does not exist, and that suffering can be avoided. Unfortunately, we know that's not true.

Sin is real. Pain is real. Death comes for each life. But death is also not the end.

We, like Mary, are standing at the foot of the cross today. Perhaps we feel separation intensely: separation from ourselves, separation from our dreams, separation from joy, separation from loved ones, separation from God.

But as Jesus' final words remind us, God is at work. God endures. Just as he entrusts his spirit to the Father, we must somehow do the same.

Good Friday is about witnessing what Christ has done for us. We stand in awe.

But by witnessing what has happened today — by hearing Jesus' words of forgiveness and comfort — by seeing him commend his spirit to God, his Father — we have not only been shown the frailty of human life, but ultimately, the power of faith.

By teaching us how to die, Jesus also teaches us how to live, so that we will never be separated from our Creator.

Resurrection of the Lord
Mark 16:1-8

The Biggest Picture of All

I have to admit that I didn't know if this was going to happen today. It was only a few years ago that we were told to stay home on Easter. That an unprecedented virus had quickly spread throughout our world, not only upending our routines, but leaving us to wonder if any sense of normal could be expected at all.

We scrambled to record and fill the airwaves, to write and fill the mailboxes; to quickly modernize through streaming technology, and go back to the time when families gathered around televisions together — this time for worship.

Despite all the fear, all the unknowns, all the warnings and restrictions, all the death and disease, we still celebrated Easter that year. I remember all the fear and fretting over if the good news would still get out there and resonate, but somehow it did. Easter refused to be stopped.

Two days ago we gathered here, and I once again wondered if today would happen. This time it wasn't the uncertainty of the pandemic that made me question Easter's arrival. No, on Friday it was fear and grief that cast their doubt on this morning.

The Friday we dare to call good offered up the holy story of betrayal and death: of the one who brought so much life suffering on a cross. How could one find hope in such a scene of misery? It was the darkness of the fading day. It was the weight of death in all its awful reality that rolled into our midst on Friday, and told its truth — of how greed and insecurity betray — of how empire executes with power and might — and of how Jesus' clear message of love for one another gets so easily dismissed and forgotten.

On Friday, it was hard to imagine that today was possible.

But we are here — on a beautiful morning — to celebrate an even more beautiful truth — that Christ is alive! That the tomb is empty! That he is risen — he is risen indeed! Alleluia!

Our gospel for today is from the book of Mark, which we have been reading all year. And like we have come to expect with Mark, it is short — and it also leaves us wanting more.

It might even leave us with some questions. You see, Mark doesn't spell out the Easter story to which we are accustomed. There are no shouts of Alleluia! There is not even an appearance by the risen Jesus.

Instead, the story is set in the half-light of sunrise, with three women going to the tomb to anoint Jesus' body. These are women who have followed Jesus. One is the woman who brought Jesus into the world: his mother Mary. These women are still shrouded in grief as they go to the tomb.

Their concerns are practical that first Easter morning: that they need someone to help them roll away the heavy stone which sits at the entrance of the tomb. Until that stone is moved, they cannot go inside and take care of Jesus' body. Until that obstacle is cleared, the story of these women and their love for Jesus cannot proceed.

When the women reach the tomb, there is a scene unlike anything they could have ever expected after Friday. The women see that the stone has already rolled back. And as they enter, they meet a young man, dressed in a white robe, sitting inside. Understandably, they are alarmed. One does not go to a tomb and expect other living people to be inside!

The young man's message is for the women to not be alarmed, but as he continues, and as he tells them that Jesus is not there in the tomb because he has been raised from the dead, the women's alarm does not subside. No, instead it grows to both terror and amazement! Rather than tell the disciples what they have seen and heard, they flee and say nothing to anyone. The final words of the Easter gospel this morning are that these women of faith are afraid.

They have seen, but they still do not see. They have heard, but they still do not understand. They have stepped inside the tomb for themselves, but grief still weighs on their hearts. Their love for Jesus has only grown in their care for him even now, and yet the pieces are not all coming together yet. The words of joy they have heard still do not yet pierce the shroud of death that weighs them down.

Obviously, this is not the end of the story. But it actually is the end of the Easter gospel in Mark. I did not skip over anything or leave any words of certainty out. This is where it stops: the tomb empty, the truth of resurrection told, the confusion and even the fear of what that all means still hanging in the air.

It might not be the perfect Easter gospel we wanted — it might not connect all the dots for us as we would like it to do — but it seems like a very fitting gospel for this time, when we have heard clearly the absolute certainty of Christ's victory over death, but we still find ourselves afraid and uncertain of what it all truly means.

A few weeks ago, I was teaching Sunday School via a computer connection. I have the confirmation-age youth in my class — young adults typically in the seventh and eighth grade. That day, through this computer-facilitated class, we had students from all over the United States in the class.

One of the joys of teaching in such a way is being able to meet students from a variety of social and church backgrounds, and having them meet each other. We have had students talk about snowstorms, bitterly cold temperatures, time spent at the beach after school, what it's like to go deer hunting, and where to get the best cheesesteak. Needless to say, it has been a great learning opportunity for me to hear these incredibly diverse conversations!

Coming from a diversity of backgrounds has also enriched how the group reads and reacts to the Bible stories we read and the lessons we learn. One week the topic of conversation was on recognizing Jesus. And I was given a series of pictures to show the students to see if they could identity what was in the photograph. It seems like a simple exercise — except that the pictures were in extreme close up, so that you saw just one tiny part of an object in detail and had to name the larger object from this small, almost microscopic, viewpoint.

Wouldn't you know — the youth did much better in this exercise than me — no surprise there! But the one picture that stumped us all was a close up with bright blue and yellow jagged stripes, with a rough texture. The students had all sorts of guesses. I figured it had to be a snake — I was certain of it, as I pointed out the bright colors and what looked like scales. But the answer key said it was a butterfly in that picture.

I apologized that the answer key must be wrong — there had to be a mistake. But one of the students said no — that there were butterflies with those colors. That their wings did have that sort of texture. That it was -indeed — a butterfly. We couldn't see it from that extreme close up viewpoint, but we could if only we stepped back. If only we could see the bigger picture.

Of course, as was revealed later in the lesson, the student was right. We were all looking at a butterfly, but the picture we had was so close to the creature that we could not imagine it to be true.

Sometimes, the answer is right there — right in front of our noses! Sometimes, the truth of creation is staring at us in the face, but we are simply unable to take in the big picture and understand. Sometimes, because of our experience of what has happened before, we find it hard to accept a new, even better truth. Sometimes, despite all of our knowledge, we simply cannot grasp the beauty of what is shouting out to us today.

Easter is here! Christ Jesus is alive! The tomb is empty because Christ has been raised and death has been defeated!

Some days that is really hard to see. And even harder to believe. Some days we need someone to point out to us the truth of the bigger picture.

We are now witnesses of these things. Whether we catch only a glimpse of resurrection today, or we see the whole picture of God's great love for all of creation — so great that even death cannot hold it, we are called to share the story with the world and be witnesses to resurrection.

Christ is risen! He is risen indeed! Alleluia!

Easter 2
John 20:19-31

Showing up to Belief

Last Sunday, after our Easter celebrations here at church, I went home and celebrated Easter with my family. Suffice it to say the Easter bunny must have injured himself carrying in the sheer weight of all that candy…

That evening, as the sugar rushes started to crash, I sat down in the living room and turned on the television, and guess which classic movie was playing? *The Wizard of Oz*. Great movie — who doesn't want to sing along to those songs and cheer on Dorothy and her gang of misfits?

And while the movie is not overtly religious, it has some universal themes in it: good versus evil, innocence versus manipulation, power versus weakness, actions versus words. That's language we use here at church, too.

And I wondered how the decision was made to play *The Wizard of Oz* on Easter. Maybe it was just because it was a holiday. Maybe there was no reason at all. Or maybe for many people, that movie does represent a sort of faith system for them. Perhaps the great wizard reminds folks of God, or the folly of chasing after idols.

And then there is the faith of Dorothy and those ruby red slippers — all brought together through the phrase: "there's no place like home." It's quaint, it's cute- that desire for the safety and innocence of home, and the belief that if we are good enough and repeat something often enough, we will believe, and our belief will make it real, and our belief will be rewarded by our wishes becoming reality.

For Dorothy, it takes a personal journey and life experience for her to realize what she's known the whole time. It takes courage and brains and a heart full of love and care for her to find out what she truly wants and believes.

It is an incredible story. How can that not resonate with us all on a personal level? That's why the movie is so good and why we still watch it. But how does it resonate with our faith?

It's one thing to come to church on Easter and hear the good news that the tomb is empty and that Jesus is risen while the choir sings, the trumpets blast, and spring flowers fill our sanctuaries. But what does it mean to really believe the good news of Easter, especially the week after Easter? Is the joy and excitement still real and present? How does the good news really enter and change our lives, and what do the rest of our days and weeks look like following our Easter experience?

Is there fear that Easter Sunday was just a big show, like the grandness of Oz's world? Can we muster together our mental willpower, click our good Sunday shoes together and somehow wish our Easter faith into existence? Can we hope that our best intentions and firmest desires somehow make the world a better place? Or are there other ways to imagine the truth of Easter taking hold in our lives for every day of our lives?

* * *

The official name might be the Second Sunday of Easter, but the unofficial name is "Low Sunday." "Low Sunday" is a way to describe the expected drop off in worship attendance following the "high" of Easter Sunday.

We probably nod along and understand why such a phenomenon would happen. After all, mountains and valleys go together. We understand that people go away on vacation. We understand that Easter is a bigger draw than the week after Easter. We understand that a drop in energy and attention is to be expected after such a momentous day.

And yet today we miss that particular joy of Easter morning. We want more of it to see, touch, hear and smell. Perhaps, in that way, we are more similar to the Apostle Thomas than we might have first imagined.

Our gospel today is known as the story of Doubting Thomas. But in a rebranding move, I would like to call it the story of the unrelenting teacher. Not only do I think we are often too hard on Thomas, but I think the great rabbi Jesus is not done teaching.

If we remember from last Sunday, early on Easter morning Jesus' resurrection is made known first to the women who come to the tomb to anoint Jesus' body. They are surprised to find an empty tomb, and it takes them a while to fully understand what has happened to their Lord.

And now, today's gospel tells us, it is evening of that very first Easter. Even though we might expect the disciples to be joyously celebrating the news of Jesus' resurrection, instead we hear they are still afraid, and remain locked in a house.

But their fear and locked doors do not stop the risen Jesus from appearing and standing amongst them. He shows the disciples his hands and his side — the wounds of his persecution and death. He offers the disciples his peace. And he breathes on them the Holy Spirit, so that they might forgive sins.

For some reason, we are not told why, Thomas is not present with the other disciples for this amazing appearance by Jesus. And so when he hears the news of what he has missed, Thomas declares that unless he sees the mark of the nails in his side, and puts his finger in the mark of the nails and his hand in Jesus' side, he will not believe.

Rather than punish Thomas for this statement, Jesus comes back a week later — this time when Thomas is present. He again stands in the midst of the disciples; he again offers peace. He invites Thomas to touch his wounds and to believe.

Certainly there is a lesson here about what it means to believe in Jesus. Blessed are those who have not seen and yet have come to believe, Jesus says. Meaning there is a blessing even for us — who have not seen — who have not touched the wounds of Jesus — and yet believe.

Jesus wants us to believe. We know this. He is the unrelenting teacher, who comes back to teach Thomas, and who has patience with all who struggle to understand and believe for themselves.

But just telling us to believe is not enough for Jesus. Jesus the teacher also shows us what belief looks like. Belief is to touch and see the very real wounds of Christ. Belief is to hear the story from others and know that it is true. Belief is to reach the place in someone's soul where they fully accept the reality of Jesus defeating death and rising to life.

Belief in Jesus is also living out lessons of forgiveness. Jesus comes back to the disciples to tell them they are to forgive others. Remember — these are the very disciples who abandoned Jesus. The very disciples who hear the fantastic news of Easter — and are still living in fear — locking themselves in a house rather than sharing the good news with the world.

To believe, Jesus seems to be teaching, is not a state of mind or a mantra we repeat again and again, but a way of life — a life of forgiving the very people who have hurt us. To believe is to share peace, even when you would probably rather be angry. To believe is to want others to believe, and not miss out on the fullness of life offered to us through the risen Jesus.

To believe in the risen Jesus is also to accept the reality of suffering. Thomas sees and touches — not just the Jesus he knew from before — but a Jesus who bears the marks of deep suffering. This is not a ghost of Jesus. It is not a vision, or a hologram, or a memory that Thomas is having. It is not just a spiritual Jesus. No, it is Jesus in bodily form, risen from death, and yet still showing his wounds.

Jesus has not forgotten what suffering feels like. And this Jesus invites Thomas to touch and see that he understands despair and darkness — that he is not afraid to go to those places of doubt and fear — and that even in the those most troubled moments, the light of Christ still shines, bringing healing of the soul and body and mind.

There is this shared, sacred moment that we witness today between Thomas and Jesus. A space created amidst the chaos of fear — where Jesus breaks through the walls of defiance that Thomas has set up around himself — so that Thomas might not only be comforted, but that he might come to proclaim, "My Lord and my God!"

Isn't that what we all seek? Somehow to make that deep spiritual connection — not only that God exists, but that God knows us — each one of us, individually. That despite all of our protests and independence, all of our defiance and self-knowledge, all of our worldly success and cries of injustice, God cares deeply for each one of us. God understands our suffering, our need. And God is able to speak to us somehow — not only that we might find comfort, but also that we might make our own confession of faith, and find our own purpose.

Thomas, as Christian legend has it, goes on to become one of the greatest evangelists of the early church. It is believed he travels to India to spread the good news of Jesus Christ — to tell others about his Lord and his God who bears the wounds of suffering and the victory of resurrection.

The crazy thing is, we also believe we have received the Holy Spirit, just like these disciples locked in the upper room. We are also often afraid of what lies out there. We are afraid of rejection, of what people might think, of failure in general. We are afraid our faith is not strong enough, or that we need a more powerful sign to truly believe like one of the disciples.

But that is simply not true.

God calls us to believe — no matter our state of belief or unbelief, perfection or imperfection, wise or foolish, brave or cowardly, full of love or searching for love. God calls us closer, so that we might find God right where we already are.

Easter 3
Luke 24:36b-48

Stories Told by Scars

When I was in the fourth grade, I had one of those unforgettable teachers that you hope every student is able to have. I remember thinking Mrs. S was ancient; she seemed to have been teaching fourth grade at our school forever. She looked and acted like a grandmother, and treated each of her students as if we were her own grandchildren.

I remember that year in her classroom for the art projects we made including one that involved painstakingly gluing different individual pieces of colored rice onto a wooden board to make a picture — which, now that I think about it, was a good way to keep students busy for a long amount of time.

I also remember that Mrs. S loved science, and when it was time to study human physiology, Mrs. S didn't just want to tell us about the digestive system. No, she insisted that we all see the scar from her gallbladder surgery so that we would know exactly where the human gallbladder was.

It was certainly a memorable day in class! In fact, to this day it is the shorthand phrase her former students use to remember what it was like to be in her class. "Do you remember Mrs. S's gallbladder scar?" is a common question whenever I encounter an old classmate.

To see her scar was to hear the story of her surgery, to learn about gallbladders, and to know that Mrs. S. was not afraid to be herself — and to teach us a lesson, even if the method was a bit odd.

Even as a child, I knew that experience of seeing a gallbladder scar was not the norm, even if it was completely innocent. After all, teachers did not typically show you their surgery scars.

Years later, when I was teaching English overseas in Namibia, I taught with a young man who only had one arm. I was told by other teachers that he had lost his arm while fighting in the country's war for independence, but I never heard that story from him.

No, I remember being afraid to ask him what had happened, how he had recovered, or how he managed to teach and go about his life now. It's not that he told me not to ask, but I assumed it was too painful to talk about such things. And so silence became another scar he had to bear.

We have been taught to hide scars. To cover them up, to pretend they don't exist, to keep them to ourselves. Even when those scars define us, and tell our stories, and are important parts of who we are.

Today's gospel is another one of the stories of Jesus after his resurrection on Easter morning. We meet him again with the disciples, giving them peace, helping them understand scripture, and even sharing a meal of fish together.

The text seems to go out of its way to prove to us readers that the risen Jesus had a body that could eat and speak and do what a normal human body does. But, of course, it is not an ordinary body, in that Jesus has a body that has come through crucifixion.

We can assume there are some visible differences apparent to the disciples in this body of Jesus in today's gospel, since they do not recognize him at first. Though not defined for us, it seems that this body is not identical, at least in appearance, to the body Jesus had before his death.

Perhaps we can understand why the disciples are startled and terrified, and why they think they are seeing a ghost. Jesus invites them to touch and see his hands and feet — the very places where his body would still carry the scars of the nails that held him to the cross.

Jesus is not ashamed of these scars; he does not try to hide them or explain them away. No, he is open in sharing the story they tell: of his suffering, death and resurrection.

The disciples also carry scars, even it their scars are not visible to us in the story. They have witnessed Jesus' betrayal and trial, his pain and death. We have to imagine that they bear the trauma of grief after witnessing the violence of the cross. They also bear other trauma, including disappointment, fear, doubt and even shame. The disciples did not expect Jesus' ministry to turn out this way, and they certainly do not always understand what has been happening.

Which is what makes Jesus' actions in today's gospel even more profound. He wants the disciples to be witnesses, and in order to be witnesses, they are to touch and see, speak with and even eat with the risen Jesus. They encounter him as a victorious Savior who still eats with them, and offers up the wounds of his suffering. In fact, it is through the wounds of his suffering that they begin to believe, to understand, and to witness to the truth they have found in the risen Christ.

* * *

So what does this gospel have to teach us today?

For early Christians, this text seems to have helped answer questions about the nature of Jesus' post-resurrection body. He did, the text tells us, have a body that could eat and speak, and still bore the wounds of his crucifixion after resurrection. Jesus was not a ghost, and not a walking-dead zombie.

And yet there is still mystery in this text, too.

While Jesus offers peace, the disciples are "startled and terrified." Jesus asks them why they doubt. Even after seeing the scars of Jesus' crucifixion, even after their joy, the disciples still struggle with their belief in what they have seen and experienced.

But Jesus does not give up on the disciples. He takes the time to explain the scriptures to them in light of the holy days they have witnessed in Jesus' suffering, death and resurrection.

It takes Jesus' patience and repeated efforts, it seems, for the disciples to truly comprehend what has happened to Jesus and to them. It takes a return to scripture to bring depth and understanding to the presence of God's holy movement. And, perhaps, Jesus' ongoing instructions to the disciples on what to do next is part of their learning experience, too.

Because once Jesus is finished explaining all that has happened, he then puts the disciples to work, sending them out as witnesses. They are to proclaim repentance and forgiveness of sins to all nations in Jesus' name. They are to start this mission in Jerusalem, but to keep pushing and extending the boundary, going and going and going far with the incredible good news of Jesus Christ.

It strikes me that the disciples are not the only ones who need more time and explanation to understand what has happened before, during and after Easter. We now have the advantage of time and distance — not only that Easter happened two weeks ago, but that we have more accounts in the New Testament and church history of how faithful followers of Jesus have continued to follow his command. People have come to believe, to experience forgiveness, to embrace new life because of the many generations who have served as faithful witnesses before us.

So why are we afraid? Why do doubts and fears still arise about whether it is worth it to us to live and repeat the good news? Why do we find it so hard some days to act as if Jesus really has defeated death and proclaimed to us peace?

It does not take us much effort or time to point out a long list of all the ways life does not seem to be consistent with Easter. War, violence and inequality dominate our headlines. In a society overflowing with too much, there are still empty tables and many who go hungry. We witness suffering, we feel pain and loss, and we carry grief in our bodies of those who no longer walk this world with us.

Considering the trauma around us, both known and unknown, we cannot even comprehend the scars that people of our community carry. But as scars tell a story, they never fully define our life's story.

As I serve as a pastor leading a church out of the pandemic, the lessons of this time are definitely ones of scars.

When news of Covid first hit, the fear of illness, the terror of the unknown, and the sudden disruption of all that was routine for us as church folks were all overwhelming. We did not know so much, and once we were able to worship, it would not be in the ways in which we had become accustomed.

We worshipped together in new ways that largely kept us separated from one another. We became good at coming together while staying apart. The sight of painter's tape marking distance on carpets and pews became normal, as were our individual profiles defined by masks. We saw each other, we might exchange a few words, but social interactions were often limited to waves from afar.

We got used to being isolated and lonely. And we had way too much practice in hiding our wounds from one another.

There have been losses, big and little, and worries we have kept to ourselves. There has been so much change, so much loss, so many griefs that we might not know where to even begin to share them with another person.

We have stood witness to the deep pain of racial division; we are fatigued by endless greed; and we have found ourselves once again shocked by unimaginable gun violence.

Our learned cultural response has perhaps been to hide the wounds of these traumas: to dismiss them and to imagine that they don't hurt, and haven't changed us.

And in doing so, we have missed out on an opportunity to witness to what God has in store for the world.

What would it mean for us to see our own wounds as a pathway to understanding? What if we could speak of our own failings as an opportunity to learn deep truths? How could our own scars tell a story of how Jesus is healing us?

This Messiah who sticks around after Easter helps us understand that it is not in spite of his scars, but through them that our faith might take shape and grow. This Savior who knows scars gives his followers the power to become witnesses to the ends of the earth.

We are called to follow: broken yet made whole in the love of our Savior.

The Sheep Life

So it happened again this week. I was out walking the dog when a stranger driving by slowed down his car and said to me, "It looks like the dog is walking you!"

I managed a half-hearted laugh. Because, of course, this stranger was right. My dog is a puller. And, after going through obedience training, I know that this is not really my dog's fault, but mine.

Dogs needs to know who the master is. Dogs need to be directed with clear commands. Dogs need to be trained to use their brains rather than their muscles and, in my dog's case, her unending stamina. Because as much as you walk her and let her run, you cannot tire my dog out. But, the trainer reassured me, you can think her out. Yes, dog psychology. Turns out I'm not very good at that either.

In order to improve the dog's behavior, we have tried different techniques with sound and collars to get her to pay attention and not pull on the leash when we walk her. But she is a dog. When she sees a bird, she thinks she can catch it. When she sees a squirrel, she wants to chase it up a tree. When she sees another dog, she pretends she's Rambo.

Which means that our walks alternate between her pulling me as fast as she can, and her stopped and unmovable, stalking her imagined prey.

It can be frustrating and time-consuming. It also feels like she is being a dog: that her instincts to hunt and scout are part of her very nature.

Perhaps, though, her instinct for loyalty is not being used to its full potential. Perhaps I, as an unsuccessful and frustrated dog walker and owner, am not living up to my human potential, either.

On this Good Shepherd Sunday we celebrate the comfort and guidance that Jesus brings us as our shepherd. In our gospel today, Jesus adopts the familiar language of the 23rd Psalm to speak of the kind of shepherd he is. Jesus is a shepherd who not only does his job in providing for and protecting the sheep in his care, but goes so far as laying down his very life for the sheep.

These poetic words of Jesus will become truth through his death and resurrection — when he brings the fullness of life — the gift of eternal life — to all of creation.

That's the big picture of the good shepherd: the one in charge of the whole herd of humanity. But this shepherd also cares for the sheep not just in a big generic sort of way, but also by knowing each and every sheep.

The Good Shepherd, we are told, knows his own, and they know him. This Good Shepherd even knows who is missing from the flock. He proclaims that he must bring the missing sheep also, and that they will listen to the shepherd's voice.

So there will be one flock, one shepherd.

Which is a beautiful image. And a reality that seems farther and farther away.

Because if we take the image of the Good Shepherd seriously, that means we are called to be sheep. Sheep who listen to the voice of the shepherd. Sheep who look to the provisions, comfort, and protection of the shepherd. Sheep who want to be gathered together. Sheep who desire that all sheep come under the care of the one shepherd whose voice they hear clearly.

Which is a beautiful metaphor for a life of faith. And also a tough sell in this world in which we live today. To be called a sheep these days is, in many circles of our society, seen as an insult. We tend to be proud of our independence, our personal opinions, our ability to not have to listen to so-called experts. And more and more, we seem to be content finding a herd that baas and nods and agrees with us in our human opinions rather than looking to the shepherd for true wisdom.

Which makes me wonder if it goes against our very human nature to be good sheep...

What does it mean for us to be called into the sheep life? I think it's helpful to go back to the kind of shepherd Jesus is. Usually the picture of Jesus with sheep is static: he is standing there, and the sheep are calm at his feet. But, in reality, a shepherd is constantly busy and engaged in some activity, having to watch the sheep, keep track of the sheep, redirect the sheep, protect the sheep, and even searching for the sheep who have left the main group.

There is constant movement, constant activity, constant call and answer — even when the sheep do not realize it.

My brothers and sisters in Christ, we have a shepherd who is relentless in his pursuit of keeping us together as a flock. He never tires and never gives up on that pursuit. No matter how often we think we know a better way; no matter how often we "baa" back, no matter how often we say we don't need a shepherd — Jesus knows that we do.

I will be honest when I say that this text has taken on greater meaning and greater challenge for me in the past few years. Not only have we witnessed great division, diverging opinions and even open hostility to people who disagree with us, but our fear of division has often paralyzed us in speaking of issues that are gospel truth to us.

Do not get me wrong: no congregation is ever going to agree on everything. There will always be disputes on which way to move and whose voice is loudest. I hope there will always be disputes on how best we can serve Jesus and love our neighbor.

We are not called into a community that has a singular voice. But we are asked to heed Jesus' vision of "one flock, one shepherd." We are called to together listen for the shepherd's voice and work in mission in such a way that the shepherd's voice is leading us.

My congregation has not been exempt from the deep political divisions of recent years. Neither was it exempt from deep political divisions of the past. But I guess what has surprised me the most over the past years is that the success stories in people coming together across great divides were often alliances I never saw coming.

When pandemic restrictions went into place, my congregation was suddenly faced with its lack of technical skill. We had a sound board no one really understood. We had no camera. While we had a social media presence, we did not post videos and did not livestream worship services.

With sudden pandemic restrictions, we also had a group of busy employed people who suddenly had time on their hands. They were eager to help, and got to work on solving a whole onslaught of problems related to providing online access to our worship services.

None of the team were experts in the field. In fact, they not only brought a wide range of backgrounds and abilities, but they also had a wide range of personalities and political beliefs. They came together to solve a problem for the church, and while they ran into more problems than I could have imagined along the way, they kept pushing for a solution.

The problems brought about an even more interesting chapter in the life of this ad hoc technology committee. Because as they talked and tinkered and tried to troubleshoot a solution to each problem, it was clear they did not agree. One would think of a particular way of fixing the solution, while another completely disagreed and wanted to attack the problem from a different angle.

As a pastor, every time this group disagreed and their voices began to rise, I was certain someone would quit in anger, and I was fearful I would be left with no group at all.

But to my great surprise, the group always worked things out on their own. I don't know why: if it was the particular people, or the particular problem they were trying to solve, or the fact that I knew so little about the technology that I completely stayed out of the discussion! But they kept trying, kept working, kept talking, kept approaching with new ideas until they inched forward, then backward, then forward again.

Their work was essential to the congregation's ministry during a time of great upheaval and forced innovation. But their friendship which came out of the work they did as a group was even more inspiring.

Here were people with very developed, distinct, and occasionally oppositional and stubborn political views who — believe it or not! — actually talked to one another! Sometimes they talked about political candidates and ideas, but most of the time they talked about music, books, movies, computers, soccer and baseball. They laughed and listened. And every once in a while they would really push each other on what and why they believed a certain thing. Even what and why they believed in God.

No, they did not have one voice. But they were one flock, whose shepherd was not a particular pastor or denomination. Neither was their shepherd a politician or celebrity. With or without saying it directly, their shepherd was Jesus Christ, who guided them in service and love of one another.

Truth be told, I do not know if this is what Jesus meant when he spoke of his vision of "one flock, one shepherd," but I think it might get close.

Our congregations are under incredible stress these days, trying to stay together and keep going when so much seems to be falling apart. How do we find common ground? How do we listen and work together when our nature is to stray?

Perhaps we might begin with humility: recognizing that we are sheep, sticking together with our herd, and listening for the shepherd's voice.

Easter 5
John 15:1-8

The Pain and Beauty of Pruning

On a beautiful spring day like today, we need to take a moment to say "thank you" to the fantastic gardeners in our world. When I walk around my neighborhood, it is obvious there are very talented and hard-working people who take beautiful care of plants all around me.

I am dazzled by blooming trees, daffodils, and irises that come back each spring, despite the harshness of the winter. I see the rich mulch placed in just the right spots around trees and plants to provide nourishment and keep out weeds. I admire shaped shrubs and bright window sills that reflect their gardener's eye for detail.

My congregation is blessed with a dedicated property crew who love to care for our outdoor spaces and truly do so in praise of God. They meticulously plant and weed, cut back and nurture forward, water and mow, edge and trim to keep everything looking just so. To sit in some of our green spaces here at church is truly a delight.

In fact, it seems there is only one blemish on our property that shows a lack of a green thumb. And that is when you are rounding the corner of the driveway. At the far end of the property, if you look to your left as you are driving past and catch a glimpse into my office window, you will notice that I am failing as a gardener.

You see, I have a big beautiful peace plant that sits in the bay window in my office. It's the perfect plant for that perfect sunny spot. Like any peace plant, that plant has been in constant bloom for years, and I have been able to enjoy it since the day I first started at my congregation. But lately it has started to put up less white blooms, and its green leaves are not the bright green they used to be.

This isn't because the plant hasn't received water or sunlight. No, it's had plenty of those basic necessities. The problem with my peace plant is me — the gardener.

Because peace plants need to be constantly pruned. They need to have the dead blooms removed, and the brown leaves cut out. They also need to have the greens thinned, so that the plant puts its energy into its graceful white blooms, rather than into producing more greenery.

It takes skill to do that — to know how and when and how much to cut out and remove from the plant so that it continues to bloom, and its leaves stay green, and for the whole plant to thrive.

And when someone like me does not care for the plant in that way, it begins to crowd itself out, and to turn brown, until there are no more blooms at all.

Pruning is an art form, really. It is also just plain work. But it is work that needs to be done if one wants to care for her plants.

Jesus says, "I am the true vine, and my Father is the vinegrower." Like any caring and talented gardener, God prunes to help the growing vines. He cuts back the branches that do not bear fruit. We do not hear of this act of pruning as a form of punishment, but so that the vines actually produce more fruit.

Pruning allows the vine to send its energy to only the branches that produce good fruit, so that the best grapes may be produced in abundance.

Of course, Jesus is not just offering gardening tips here. He is speaking of our connection to the holy. We are to cut what does not produce good fruit of the Spirit. So that when the nonproductive stuff in our lives is trimmed away, we may intensify our connection to God and produce even better fruit.

But as we know, pruning is for the skilled gardener. Some branches might be really good at making great big green leaves, but they might not be good at making fruit. And while we might be drawn to the big green leafy branches, and might want to keep those green leafy branches, God the gardener knows to look for the fruit hidden under the leaves.

So we get this gardening metaphor Jesus uses today: we know pruning is good, and that pruning helps the plant. Why, then, are we sometimes reluctant to prune?

Perhaps we are afraid we will cut the wrong branches. Perhaps we simply do not want to cut down the branches that are leafy and lush.

And if we switch this metaphor to us as Jesus does— if we are the branches — then we know pruning hurts. And we are reluctant at what might be lost.

Recently my husband's grandmother passed away at the age of 95. We called her Nanny, and she lived a great life: from the Roaring Twenties, through the Depression and World War II, and all the way to welcoming great grandchildren into her life and being able to teach them the wonders of homemade chocolate cake with white icing.

Unfortunately the last ten years of her life were marked by progressive dementia, which is a disease that I really struggle to understand. It is so hard to watch someone you love — someone so full of stories and memories and love — slowly disappear, a bit at a time. We watched as she lost her desire to socialize, her cognitive function, and finally her physical capacities — one branch at a time — in a slow and unrelenting progression.

At first we noticed that she would repeat stories — sometimes telling us the same memory only moments after the story had just finished. She started eating less, and didn't like cooking at home anymore. We watched as she began to forget tasks she was supposed to do and skills she used to have.

Then she forgot words and the names of places she liked to go. Until she forgot our names, and, finally, she forgot our faces, too.

To watch someone you love suffer from dementia feels like a cruel pruning of their lives. They lose so much — and in turn, you lose so much, too. It's hard not to focus on the losses — on those branches that have been cut that used to be so lush and green.

But whatever is connected to God thrives, Jesus tells us. And while it didn't take away all the pain at what was lost, there were moments even late into her disease that showed us she was still connected to what was important. She would light up at a single chocolate chip cookie. She would look 300 times at pictures of trips she took 30 years ago, and still be excited, as if the trip had just happened yesterday. She beamed at something as simple at seeing her great grandchildren walk into the room to visit her.

The fruits that had been so little we hardly noticed them became the fruits that connected us to her — and we knew they were gifts from God.

Make no mistake — pruning hurts. To lose anything is painful. To lose anyone is unbearable. I wish I could understand the whys and hows and whats of pruning, and exactly what Jesus means in this gospel today.

But I do know that we are not the gardener. What a relief that we are not the gardener! Even if from our perspective, it is impossible to understand why the gardener prunes this branch and not that one. We are still assured that the gardener cares for the vine and its fruit.

As we enter into what feels like a new time — for us, for our congregation, for the larger church, and for our world — it feels like we have been pruned. As people of faith, we know the pruning will continue.

We are called to keep growing — not judging growth by what is lush in our eyes, but what produces fruit for God's kingdom.

Somehow — in all of this — we know that the source of all life comes from God — and that this connection to what is eternal will sustain us through all the losses of life. Just like all of our brothers and sisters in Christ, we are branches of the true vine.

Pictures of Love

Schedule master. Taxi driver. Maker of hot cereal on cold winter mornings. Nurse, with an expertise in removing splinters. Comforter. Listener of all woes. The one who can fix anything that is wrong. Master book reader. Washer of enormous mountains of laundry. Cookie baker extraordinaire. The one incapable of making any less than a refrigerator-bottom-drawer-crisper full of potato salad.

That was the picture — or pictures -I had of my mother when I was child. She was a great source of love and affection, and also a great task-master related to all the jobs I needed her to do for me!

Which is why I was always so shocked when I went to visit my grandmother. Like most grandmothers, my grandma had lots of pictures in her house of me (of course!) and of my siblings. She was proud of us, and seemed to have both saved and displayed every school picture, Christmas card, and art project we had ever made and given to my grandmother.

But that wasn't the full extent of everything one could view in her personal gallery. No, in my grandmother's house, she had an entire hallway of pictures of her daughter, my mother. Pictures of my mother as a baby, and as a young girl. School pictures from when my mother had been a student. And pictures of my mother as a teenager and young woman.

Can you believe my mother used to be a teenager? Can you believe she used to drive a car that was not a minivan? Can you imagine a time that she wasn't my mother?

It sounds strange, but I really couldn't. When I was a child, it was eye-opening to imagine that my mother had been the same age as me — that she had not always known what she wanted to do with her life.

That she had listened to music that was not considered "oldies" at the time. That she had her own teenage rebellion years.

I would stare at those pictures of my young mother when I was visiting my grandmother, and try to wrap my mind around my mother's life before me. And it was sort of impossible for me to do that. Not only because I was all about the stuff my mother did for me, but also because I defined her in relationship to myself rather than all the many other people to whom she was connected.

It was a challenge — to at least try to imagine how my grandmother saw my mother — and to look at those pictures through her eyes.

Our gospel this week is a continuation of last Sunday's passage on God as vine. We are asked to abide in God's love again this week — not only because Jesus asks us to do that, but because Jesus knows this is the way to truly live.

If we abide in God's love — if we keep Jesus' commandments to love one another — then we will flourish, finding joy and producing good fruit. Our lives will be connected to the source of all life. And having experienced such grace and love in Jesus Christ, we will be able to offer grace and love in return.

That all sounds right on par with what Jesus said last week in talking about the vine and branches and fruit. God the gardener is somehow able to prune in such a way that the fruits of the kingdom might flourish.

But then Jesus says something that catches my ears in a new way this week: something that I do not quite expect, to be honest. Jesus adds to this image of the vine and this story of love. Yes, Jesus adds a new perspective by calling his disciples friends. He says, "I do not call you servants any longer, because the servant does not know what the master is doing; but I have called you friends, because I have made known to you everything that I have heard from my Father. You did not choose me but I chose you."

Jesus calls us friends. Jesus, in fact, says he chose us to be his friends.

Now in the text we get some additional understanding of what this means. Friendship for Jesus means love that is willing to lay down one's life for one's friends. And we know that Jesus will do this in the most extreme form of love possible. Indeed, we know that he will go to the cross in order to give us life.

What is amazing to me is that when Jesus says these words — the very same words on love and friendship echoing in our ears today —

the setting is actually the Lord's Supper, the night of his betrayal and death. These words are part of his farewell: his final instructions to the disciples on how they are to live in his absence.

Even though the disciples will abandon and deny and betray, Jesus still lays down his life for them. It does not seem like a very reciprocal relationship, does it? It does not sound like a very equal friendship. It does not appear that Jesus gets too much out of this friendship compared to what he gives.

Why in the world does Jesus choose these disciples as friends? Why in the world does he call us friends, too?

One of the ironies of Mother's Day is that we celebrate impossible standards for parents. We imagine our mothers and fathers are superheroes, and they are superheroes in many ways. But what we celebrate can also come across as expectation.

Thank you for keeping band and sports uniforms clean! Thank you for making endless meals, continually replenishing food in the refrigerator and cabinets, and washing dishes until your hands crack! Thank you for serving as taxi driver!

The list could go on and on.... Being a parent is not easy. Being a parent is also one of the most rewarding roles in the world.

Perhaps rather than focus on the tasks that parents "do" for us, we might somehow stress the importance of the relationship itself. Sons and daughters need a teacher. They need a safety patrol who sets and keeps boundaries. They need a good listener. They need a judge who carries both justice and mercy. They need a source of unconditional love.

I know — those are even more impossibly high standards than keeping up with the piles of laundry and dirty dishes. But in focusing on those roles, we might see how a congregation can help parents.

Can church members not just stop kids from running in the narthex, but explain to them what the sanctuary means to them? Do we give time to offer the name of our favorite worship song, and ask young people what their favorite song is, and why? Can we open the Bible and read along with our pew mate, helping with the hard words and being brave enough to engage in difficult questions to which we might now know the answer?

It is beyond the scope of parenting, perhaps, but I would argue it is within the parameters of friendship. And perhaps churches have something to offer when it comes to friendship. Not only in the gospel text we receive today, but in the models of church we know and cherish, where we check in on one another, share one another's joys, bear one another's burdens, and generally help one another to be the Body of Christ together.

"What a Friend We Have in Jesus" is one of my favorite hymns. I love singing it. I love the imagery and the idea that Jesus is my friend. That I can count on him. That he is with me in good times and bad. I can go on and on and still not speak to all the ways in which Jesus is a friend to us.

So it makes sense that I should also launch into a laundry list of what we should do in return. The ways we ought to love one another. The fruit we are called to produce when we abide in the vine. The list is long. And I know I am falling short.

If we are to imagine our friendship with Jesus as an equal platform, there is no way we could measure up. Any comparison of our accomplishments, our fulfillment of a to-do list, or the depths of our commitment, simply do not come close to the deep love Jesus has for us. That might feel like failure.

But here we are. Here is Jesus today calling us friends. And I wonder if we might be able to try and see ourselves as Jesus sees us: with eyes full of grace, choosing to call us friends.

What if we could see our brothers and sisters in Christ with the same eyes of grace? What if we could see our neighbors with grace? What if we could look at all of our fellow pilgrims here on Earth as friends: walking this journey together. We each have our particular fragilities, our bumps and bruises, our need for grace, and our own unique ability to serve.

For each one of us, God chooses to reach out with a hand of friendship. It is ours to grasp and hold on to so that we might be blessed in holy friendship forever.

Jesus' Prayer for Us

Perhaps you are aware of the term "life hack." A life hack is a tip someone gives to make life easier. Often the tips are quite simple, and sometimes they are even obvious. But ideally, they are ways of doing things that we just never thought of before. When someone shows us such a life hack, we are able to go about our daily routine in a new, hopefully easier, way.

Need an icepack that doesn't drip? Put a frozen saturated sponge in a sealed bag. Want to avoid drips while eating a popsicle? Fit a cupcake liner around the bottom of the frozen treat. Are you removing the stems of strawberries and want to waste as little as possible? Use a straw to pop out the stem from the bottom.

Perhaps these life hacks seem a bit silly. But if we try them and find they work, we will likely adopt them into our routine. Hopefully, we will even save some time, energy and aggravation in the process!

Social media is full of these life hacks. In fact, people try to attract followers on various sites by highlighting their own life hacks to help other people.

And while many life hacks are simple and straightforward and helpful, some seem pretty odd, at least at first. For example, I do not really want to make food in my kitchen sink (no thanks). And the idea of never washing my blue jeans — ever — just doesn't seem right to me.

So while I will never follow all the life hacks that are popular on social media, there are definitely some that I can include in my daily routine. And when someone shows us a way of life that improves our own, we cannot imagine going back to the old way we did things.

Because part of the fun in trying out these "life hacks" is the reactions you get from people around you. If we grew up cutting strawberries a certain way, if we "always did it that way," and suddenly someone shows up pushing out the stems with a straw, we wonder what in the world is happening.

It is almost funny to see how tied to certain notions of "the right way" we have become, and how hard it is to change in our habits. I guess that is part of the appeal of a life hack — the shock that another way of doing something has been right there in front of us the whole time.

To embrace a new way of doing something is to wonder if perhaps we do not have a monopoly on "the right way." It is to ask, "Why does everyone knowing something make it right?" Or, to flip the question around, it is to consider if we are able to imagine a truth that the world does not yet embrace.

I have found that trying a new way of doing something can also start a conversation about why we do things the way we do. That by challenging the status quo — and, more importantly — by trying to understand how someone else sees the world — can lead us to a truth we had never imagined before. And, in the process of embracing a new truth, we are changed, too.

Most life hacks promoted on social media are about pretty simple daily tasks that do not radically change the world around us. But challenging accepted truth is not just the realm of social media influencers. No, as Christians we follow one who challenged the entire world's understanding of truth. He knew the consequences; he knew the persecution that was to come from such truth; and yet Jesus called us into a truth that leads to life.

* * *

I'll be honest: on a first read, today's gospel sounds like a hot mess. It's hard to understand exactly what's going on. It's difficult to extract from it any quick and easy message that can motivate us for the week ahead.

What we get instead of a clear instructional manual or inspiring remarks is a muddled prayer. And just like when we pray, Jesus' prayer is not exactly clear and linear. No, it is emotional — from the heart just as much as from the head — a bit repetitive and confusing to those listening from the outside. But the message is still obvious to the disciples: Jesus is connected directly to God the Father, and, now through this prayer, they hear that Jesus prays that the disciples and all who follow Jesus might also be connected in such a close way to God.

Our reading this week happens just before Jesus' crucifixion. Jesus knows he is about to leave this world — he knows the challenges and suffering he is about to face — and yet his prayer is focused on others — that we might enjoy the same close relationship with God that he has with the Father.

Jesus reveals that being included in this truth that comes from God means that the world is a hostile place. It is not easy to follow the way of God. In fact, if we do — if we accept God's word — Jesus says we will not belong to the world.

In other words, if we don't feel the world is against us, we're not doing it right.

How's that for motivation this week?! Not very encouraging, is it?! And yet if we really take this gospel seriously — if we really want to follow Jesus — we are choosing the path of most resistance in life. We are believing a truth that will always go against what everyone else accepts as true.

It doesn't mean we accept everyone's opinion as truth. It means we accept the radical, world-challenging teachings of Jesus as truth: that forgiveness is holy work, that love can change the world, that there is no person beyond the scope of God's grace — including ourselves. Following Christ means we choose to live in such a way that shows we actually believe these truths — not in spite of how difficult they are, but precisely because Jesus has declared that the world needs to be changed.

Too many times in our history, we have thought that following Jesus' truth meant we were to draw lines in the sand.

In Jesus' time, good, religious people believed that Samaritans were enemies; that tax collectors were beyond the scope of God's grace; that lepers should never be touched or even allowed into the town. Good religious people who encountered Jesus truly believed that there were people that they had to avoid in order to stay holy.

The trend continued. Some of Jesus' own disciples believed that Gentiles could not possibly receive the good news of Jesus Christ. Wars have been fought in endless succession over who was right about how to worship God and on whose side God sent blessing and victory.

Our truth — the truth we twist and turn for our own use and to make ourselves look good — only leads to more defeat until we meet God's truth.

God's story — and through God, our story — is that over and over and over again — just when we thought we understood where to draw a line to keep out who was wrong and make ourselves right, God proves us wrong. The Spirit pushes the boundary, constantly challenging us, and continually reminding us that God has a much larger dream for the world than we could ever imagine.

I wonder sometimes if we believe that. If we can believe in God's great truth? It is not easy when we would rather accept easy truths the world teaches: that there will never be peace in our world; that loneliness is part of human existence; that we must just get used to the pain of racism, the fear of scarcity, rampant greed, and great inequalities.

But we have seen God's truth. We have heard Jesus' prayer for us. And we are called not only to believe, but to live in such a way that the world will know we have found the Truth.

Remember that Jesus' words of good news today are all in the form of a long prayer. Meaning that the work of God continues, just as long as this prayer continues to be read and listened to and prayed again every time we hear it.

Just as Jesus prayed for us — for all of us still in this world — the life of this good news goes on. And we pray knowing that Jesus' truth is ours forever.

Day of Pentecost
John 15:26-27; 16:4b-15

New Life Through Fire

Omwene, kwoove ou Nda djuulukwa

The first time I heard it, I didn't understand either.

I was at Oshigambo Lutheran Church in Oshigambo, Namibia, where I was teaching English at the Lutheran High School down the road. And since I was in Namibia representing the church, I thought I should probably go to church.

Worship in rural Namibia at that time was not a quick item to check off your list for the week — it was a full day experience. People would walk hours to go to church, bringing their lunch and dressed in their Sunday best. And although there was a start time to worship, the pastor would not begin the service until he determined enough people had arrived.

Just like a service here, the pastor would give announcements, there was liturgy and readings, a sermon and offering — sometimes multiple offerings if the offering wasn't enough the first time — and there was lots of singing out of the hymnal.

Everything was in Oshindonga, the local language. Which meant I did not understand too much of what was being said. Sometimes a person would offer to translate for me and help me through the service, but many times I learned to just sit, let the sound wash over me, and take in what I could.

I could follow the flow of the service. I also could not help but be moved by the hymns. With no organ and no piano in this rural church, music was led by just a song leader who would stand, call out the number of the hymn, and lead the singing. This happened in a very predictable fashion: after giving the first note, the entire congregation would then join in with full force, adding their own harmonies to the simple melody line that was found in the hymnal.

Even I could understand the power of these hymns, even if I could not understand the words.

This went on for many Sundays. Some days I went to church because I knew they were expecting to see me. Some mornings I went because I wanted to hear the singing. Some days I wondered why I went when I couldn't understand what was being said.

And then one day, during a hymn, I realized that I recognized the tune. It was not quite the way I had grown up singing it back in Minnesota, but yes — it was the golden oldie, "Nearer my God to Thee."

It turns out the hymnal used at the church in Oshigambo had many hymns brought over by Finnish missionaries in the 1800s — including what was a contemporary hymn at the time, "Nearer my God to Thee." A hymn written by the English poet Sarah Flower Adams about the Old Testament character Jacob, an ancient dreamer. Jacob's story is of wandering, his journey to find God, and his dream that God was indeed near to him, no matter how far he strayed. (Sourced from www.hymnary.org.)

Here was a church full of people singing in Oshindonga,

Omwene, kwoove ou Nda djuulukwa — words we can all understand.

Sometimes, through the loud noise this world makes, God's voice still breaks through. Somehow, through all of our doubt that God could ever speak to us, we know that God has drawn us close. Some day, through all the misunderstanding and confusion of peoples, God will help us see how we are connected through the Spirit of the Holy.

The story of Pentecost is one of spectacular confusion and wild understanding. The apostles know that the Advocate is coming — Jesus himself told them this Spirit of God would arrive to them in Jerusalem soon — and yet it had to be terrifying when the Spirit's arrival actually happened, with tongues of fire and the sound of the rush of a violent wind.

The crowd of people in Jerusalem that day, from different cultures and languages, are all able to hear and understand God's deeds of power. And Peter is able to capture the power of the moment, recalling the ancient words of the prophet Joel about visionaries and dreamers, and connecting the treasured words of the past to the life of Jesus Christ and the power of the Spirit in their midst right then and there.

It is as if the stars align and the dots connect. Not only does the Holy Spirit arrive, but the people recognize its power, and Peter is able to give voice to God's word. It is this spectacular point in time when God is also able to seize the full attention of all those gathered together that day — so that they know a new time has come. They are no longer people who cannot understand. They are no longer people who are waiting for God's Spirit. They are no longer people clouded by misunderstanding. Now God holds them together as one people who can understand one another and hear God speak.

To read the story of Pentecost is to imagine the wonder of this moment. To hear the story of Pentecost is also to believe that the Holy Spirit still blows, still works, still speaks, still can move us — even if we do not always understand every word.

I often find myself waiting for the clarity of Pentecost to arrive in one fell swoop in front of me. I would like a crystal clear understanding both of God's Word, and of how we are called to be God's people together. I would love to immediately be able to speak the language of my neighbor, and more importantly, that I could understand the other so that there would be no division between us. Instead, in my waiting, I often find myself asking the question of the crowd that day: "What does this mean?"

And in asking that question, I believe we are seeking and inviting the Spirit.

One of the traditions of my denomination is to have the service of confirmation on Pentecost Sunday. Just as we celebrate the Holy Spirit's arrival, we pray for the Holy Spirit to confirm lives of holy witness and call our young adults into even greater service in the world.

But I laugh because one of the other traditions in my congregation is that young adults being confirmed do not have to serve as acolytes the day of their confirmation.

It seems like it should be a very small problem, and yet many times I am scratching my head as to who will now fill this role.

You see, part of their training and education before being approved for confirmation is to assist with worship. In particular, confirmation students are to assist in acolyting duties. This means they gather items during holy communion, help with the offering plates, and both light the candles at the beginning of worship and put them out again at the conclusion of worship.

To add to the excitement, they even get to sit in a special pew up front! Yippee! (This is excitement definitely not shared by my confirmation students...)

Unfortunately, in addition to the extreme boredom my students seem to share in having to listen to my sermons with the entire congregation noticing if they fall asleep or not, maintaining the flame for lighting the candles is also a source of great stress for our young people. Walking down the aisle at the beginning of worship, they fret that the flame they are carrying might be extinguished, and that they will be forced to walk back to the usher, have their wick re-lit, and then have to walk down the aisle all over again — all with the entire congregation staring at them, or so they assume.

The wick going out is a common occurrence, made even more common when the fans are on in the sanctuary. The acolytes, so they tell me, feel they are forced to walk through a wind tunnel with the entire congregation watching.

They might be exaggerating just a bit, but I understand their fear and frustration. I also understand that an essential part of fire is that it cannot be completely controlled. Even when we carefully monitor our wicks, and cradle our flames, and try to avoid wind; even when we hold our breath, and watch over flames carefully, and fret over who is watching us carry the flame — even then, there is still something about this fire we dare to control that defies us and does at it pleases.

This is very frustrating for a young acolyte who is convinced the entire world is staring at them and judging them. But in God's hands, holy fire's ability to dance and dream and defy our expectations is indeed a great gift.

Perhaps one of the greatest frustrations shared by churches right now is that we sense that the system that has seemingly worked for us for so long is not working so well anymore. We might experience frustration at declining attendance, a lack of volunteers, or simply sadness that the church we remember from years past no longer exists.

We might even be angry that our status in the community has declined, or that others do not value the church culture and traditions the way we do. On the other hand, we might be equally frustrated and upset that our congregation is not open to change the way we would like them to be, or the way we imagine ourselves to be.

For each and all of us, the Holy Spirit blows. It rattles our old ways and it breaks down divisions between peoples. It arrives as wind and flame, stirring every heart and causing us to speak languages we never spoke before, and understand other people who we never understood before.

It can blow in like wildfire, or sometimes arrives one word at a time, and remains a mystery — this vast unknown that I can only see a tiny piece of. We still have no idea of the vastness of God's language, and of God's love for all people. But we keep going, trying to understand, knowing that God understands us and sees our hearts.

We pray, trusting fully that there are common links joining us to other people — even people who seem so very different to us, who perhaps struggle to understand the language of faith we speak.

No matter what, the Holy Spirit does not stop: despite our protests, despite our best efforts to control it, despite our fear of what will happen when holy fire burns.

Somehow, Pentecost catches us by surprise yet again, as fire brings new life to tired bones and worn institutions, and holy excitement to our young and adventurous. We speak in a new language today, as we welcome God's presence amongst us.